The Secret Language of Crime:

Vocabulum or the Rogue's Lexicon

GEORGE W. MATSELL

COSIMOCLASSICS

NEW YORK

The rogue fraternity have a language peculiarly their own, which is understood and spoken by them no matter what their dialect, or the nation where they were reared. Many of their words and phrases, owing to the comprehensive meaning, have come into general use, so that a Vocabulum or Rogue's Lexicon, has become a necessity to the general reader, but more especially to those who read police intelligence.

—from the Preface

PREFACE

When a young man enters upon the business of life, he may have some indefinite idea of what he intends to follow out to the close thereof; but he soon finds himself surrounded by circumstances which control his actions and business pursuits, and lead him into channels of thought and industry that had not previously entered into his philosophy. At least I have found it to be so, and I have no doubt others have had a similar experience. To become a lexicographer, certainly never entered into my calculation, or even found a place in the castle-building of my younger days; and if a kind friend had suggested to me that I was destined to fill such a position in life, I would simply have regarded him as a fit subject for the care of the authorities. This improbable event has now taken place; and I present myself to the world as the compiler of a language used in all parts of the world, and yet understood connectedly but by few persons.

The rogue fraternity have a language peculiarly their own, which is understood and spoken by them no matter what their dialect, or the nation where they were reared. Many of their words and phrases, owing to the comprehensive meaning, have come into general use, so that a Vocabulum or Rogue's Lexicon, has become a necessity to the general reader, but more especially to those who read police intelligence.

Occupying the position of a Special Justice, and Chief of the Police of the great Metropolis of New York, where thieves and others of a like character from all parts of the world congregate, and realizing the necessity of possessing a positive knowledge of every thing connected with the class of individuals with whom it was my duty to deal, I was naturally led to study their peculiar language, believing that it would enable me to converse with them more at ease, and thus acquire a knowledge of their character, besides obtaining from them information that would assist me in the position I occupied, and consequently be of great service to the public. To accomplish this task was no mean undertaking, as I found that it required years of diligent labor to hunt up the various authorities, and these when found proved only partially available, as much of the language in present use was unwritten, and could only be obtained by personal study among first-class thieves who had been taught it in their youth. The difficulties surrounding it, did not deter me from following out my resolution, and by closely pursuing it, I had opened up to me a fountain of knowledge that I could not have obtained if I had not possessed a clear understanding of this peculiar dialect. Experience has since demonstrated to me that any man engaged in police business can not excel without understanding the rogues' language, in the study of which they will find this Lexicon of invaluable service.

It is not, however, to policemen alone that this book will be of service, as these cant words and phrases are being interwoven with our language and many of them are becoming recognized Anglicisms. It is not unusual to see them in the messages of presidents and governors — to hear them enunciated at the bar and from the pulpit, and thus they have come to be acknowledged as appropriately expressive of particular ideas; so that while they are in common use among the footpads that infest the land, the *élite* of the Fifth Avenue pay homage to their worth, by frequently using them to express thoughts, that could not, otherwise, find a fitting representative. The vocabulary of the rogue is not of recent date, although it is mainly made up of arbitrary or technical words and phrases, while others are of a purely classical origin. It is a language of great antiquity, and may be dated back to the earliest days of the roving gipsy bands, that infested Europe, from whom the greater portion of it has been derived. It might more properly be termed the Romany or Gipsy language, adapted to the use of modern rogues in all parts of the world, and in which the etymologist will find words drawn from every known language. Some of these words are peculiarly national, but as a general thing the language of the rogue in New York is the language of the rogue the world over.

Among policemen, not only in this city but in different parts of the United States, the cant language of thieves is attempted to be used; but there being no standard they are unable to do so understandingly, and each one gives to the words the corrupted sense in which he received it; thus speaking as it were, a miserable *"patois,"* to the ex-

8

clusion of the true "Parisian French." This departure from the true meaning of the words used is mischievous in its tendency, as it is calculated to mislead and bewilder, so that rogues might still converse in the presence of an officer, and he be ignorant of what they said. This I have endeavored to correct, and although I may not claim infallibility in these matters, yet I believe that I have arrived at as high a degree of perfection as is now attainable.

To the readers of the *National Police Gazette,* the oldest and most reliable criminal journal published in the United States, this work will prove invaluable, as it will enable them to understand and fully comprehend language that the editors and correspondents are frequently compelled to use in order to convey the idea as understood by rogues in general.

GEO. W. MATSELL.
New York, 1859.

A

ABRAHAM To sham; to pretend sickness.

ABRAHAM COVE A naked or poor man; a beggar in rags.

ACADEMY A penitentiary, or prison for minor offenses.

ACCOUNTS To cast accounts; to vomit.

ACE OF SPADES A widow.

ACKRUFFS River-thieves; river-pirates.

ACORN A gallows.

ADAM An accomplice; a pal.

ADAM-TYLER A fellow whose business it is to receive the plunder from the "File" — the one who picked the pocket — and get away with it.

ACTEON A cuckold.

ACTIVE CITIZEN A louse.

ADDLE-COVE A foolish man.

AGOG Anxious; impatient; all-agog.

AGOGARE Anxious; eager; impatient; be quick.

AIR AND EXERCISE To work in the stone quarry at Blackwell's Island or at Sing Sing.

ALAMORT Confounded; struck dumb; unable to say or do any thing.

ALBERT A chain.

ALBONIZED Whitened.

ALLS The five alls. First, the monarch's motto, "I govern all." Second, the bishop's motto, "I pray for all." Third, the lawyer's motto, "I plead for all." Fourth, the soldier's motto, "I fight for all." Fifth, the farmer's motto, "I pay for all."

ALTEMAL All in a heap, without items; the sum total.

ALTITUDES A state of drunkenness; being high.

AMBIDEXTER One who befriends both sides; a lawyer who takes fees from both parties in a suit.

AMERACE Very near; don't go far; be within call.

AMPUTATE YOUR MAHOGANY OR TIMBER Be off quick; away with you.

AMUSE To amuse; to invent plausible stories and thereby rob or cheat unsuspecting persons.

AMUSERS Fellows who carry snuff or pepper in their pockets, which they throw into a person's eyes and then run away; the accomplice rushing up to the victim, pretending to assist, robs him while suffering with pain.

ANGLERS Small thieves who place a hook on the end of a stick, and therewith steal from store-windows, doors,

11

etc. It also applies to fencemen; putters up, etc.

ANOINTED Flogged.

ANKLE "A sprained ankle;" the mother of a child born out of wedlock.

ANODYNE Death; to anodyne, to kill. "Ahr say, Bill, vy don't yer hopen that jug and draw the cole?" "Vy, my cove, aren't you avare as how a bloke snoses hin it?" "Vell, vot hof it, aren't yer habel to put him to hanodyne?"

APPLES AND PEARS Stairs.

AQUA Water.

ARCH-COVES Chief of the gang or mob; headmen; governors; presidents.

ARCH-DUKE A funny fellow.

ARCH-GONNOFF The chief of a gang of thieves.

ARD Hot.

ARK A ship; a boat; a vessel.

ARTFUL DODGERS Lodgers; fellows who dare not sleep twice in the same place for fear of arrest.

ARTICLE Man. "You're a pretty article." A term of contempt.

ARTICLES A suit of clothes.

ARTIST An adroit rogue.

ASSAY Go on; commence; try it.

ATTLEBOROUGH Not genuine; made to imitate. At the town of Attleborough jewelry is manufactured from the baser metals, or so alloyed as to de-

ceive those who are not good judges of
the genuine article.

AUTUM A church.

AUTUM-BAWLER A parson.

AUTUM-DIVERS Pickpockets who
practise in churches.

AUTUMED Married.

AUTUM-COVE A married man.

AUTUM-CACKLER A married
woman.

AUTUM-JET A parson.

AWAKE To know; to let know.

B

BABY PAPS Caps.

BACONNING A fat round face; a full pale face.

BADGER A panel thief; a fellow who robs a man's pocket after he has been enticed into bed with a woman; to torment.

BAGGED Imprisoned.

BAG OF NAILS Every thing in confusion.

BALL Prison allowance.

BALLUM-RANCUM A ball where all the dancers are thieves and prostitutes.

BALSAM Money.

BAM A lie; to bamboozle; humbug.

BANDERO A widow's weeds.

BANDOG A civil officer.

BANGUP The best; very fine; height of the fashion.

BAPTIZED Liquor that has been watered.

BARDY A sixpence.

BARKER One who patrols the streets for customers in front of his employer's shop; vide Chatham street.

BARKING Shooting.

BARKING-IRONS Pistols.

BARNACLES A good booty; a pair of spectacles; hand-cuffs.

BARREL FEVER Delirium tremens.

BASTER A house-thief.

BAT A prostitute who walks the streets only at night.

BAZAAR A counter.

BEAK A magistrate; a judge.

BEAKQUERE A sharp, strict magistrate who is attentive to his duty.

BEAT Get the best of him; "Beat the flat;" rob the man.

BEATERS }
BEATER-CASES } Boots.

BEAU-TRAPS Well-dressed sharpers; fortune-hunters.

BEANS Five-dollar gold-pieces.

BELCHER TIE A flashy neckerchief.

BEN A vest.

BENE Good; first rate.

BENE-BOUSE Good drink.

BENE-COVE A good man.

BENEN-COVE A better man.

BENE-CULL A good fellow.

BENE-DARKMAN Good night.

BENDER A spree; a drunken frolic.

BENFLAKE A cheap beef-steak.

BENISON A blessing.

BENJAMIN A coat.

BENS Fools.

BESS A pick of a very simple construction.

BETSEY *See Bess.*

BETTING HIS EYES A term used by gamblers when a "sucker" looks on at the game, but does not bet.

BETTY A picklock.

BEVER An afternoon lunch.

BIENLY Excellently, "She coaxed so bienly."

BIG THING A rich booty.

BILBOA A pointed instrument.

BILK To cheat.

BILLY A piece of whalebone or raw-hide about fourteen inches long, with an oval-shaped lump of lead at each end, one larger than the other, the whole being covered with buckskin or india-rubber.

BILLY BUTTER Mutton.

BILLY NOODLE A soft fellow that believes the girls are all in love with him.

BILL OF SALE A widow's weeds.

BINGAVAST Get you gone, "Bing we to New York;" go we to New York.

BINGO Liquor.

BINGO-BOY A drunken man.

BINGO-MORT A drunken woman.

BIRDLIME Time. Time arrests and reveals all things.

BIRTHDAY SUIT Stark naked.

BIT Out-witted, "The cove was bit;" "The cove has bit the flat, and pinched his cole," outwitted and robbed him.

BIT Done; sentenced; convicted.

BITE To steal; to rob.

BLACK ACT Picking locks.

BLACK-BOX A lawyer.

BLACK FRIARS Lookout.

BLACK OINTMENT Raw meat.

BLACK SPY The devil.

BLACKLEG A gambler.

BLARNEY A picklock.

BLEAK Handsome; "The Moll is bleak," the girl is handsome.

BLEAK-MORT A pretty girl.

BLEATING RIG Sheep-stealing.

BLEED To compel a person to give money under threat of exposure.

BLINK Not to see when one may. "The copper blinks, and won't drop to me," i.e. the officer pretends not to see me; the officer looks another way. To go to sleep.

BLOCK-HOUSE A prison.

BLOWEN The mistress of a thief. "The blowen kidded the bloke into a panel crib, and shook him of his honey and thimble," i.e. the girl enticed the man into a thieving-house, and robbed him of his watch and money.

BLOW A CLOUD Smoke a segar or pipe.

BLOKE A man.

BLOTTED Written.

BLOW To inform.

BLOSS Woman; mistress; girl.

BLUDGET A female thief who decoys her victims into alley-ways, or other dark places, for the purpose of robbing them.

BLUDGEONER A fellow who passes off some well-dressed woman as his wife. She goes out in search of a gallant, and entices her victim into some unfrequented place. The bludgeoner waits outside until she gives him a signal that the man is robbed, when he rushes in with a knife, pistol, or club, and accuses the man with having seduced his wife. The poor fool gets away as fast as possible, and does not know that he is robbed.

BLUE-BILLY A peculiar handkerchief.

BLUE-PIGEON-FLYING Stealing lead off the tops of houses.

BLUE-PLUM A bullet; "Surfeit the bloke with blue-plum," shoot him.

BLUE-RUIN Bad gin.

BLUFF To bluster; look big.

BLUFFER The landlord of a hotel.

BLUNDERBUSS An ignorant, blustering fellow.

BLUNT Money.

BOARDING-HOUSE City prison; the Tombs.

BOARDING-SCHOOL Penitentiary.

BOAT "To boat with another;" to go in with him; to be his partner in the same boat — in the same scrape.

BOATED Transported; gone to sea.

BOB The fellow that caries off the plunder; a shoplifter; a cover or staller.

BOBBIE A policeman.

BOB-CULL A good fellow.

BOB MY PAL My girl.

BODY-COVER A coat.

BOGUS Bad coin; false.

BOKE The nose.

BOLT Run away.

BONE To take; to steal; to ask him for it.

BONEBOX The mouth.

BONED Arrested; taken; carried off.

BONESETTER A hard-riding horse.

BONNET Hat. "Bonnet him," knock his hat down over his eyes.

BONNETTER One who entices another to play; or the fellow who takes the "flat" in hand after the "roper in" has introduced him to the house.

BOOTH A place in which thieves congregate.

BOOSING-KEN A drinking-shop.

BOODLE A quantity of bad money.

BOODLE-CARRIER The man who carries the bulk of the counterfeit money that is to be passed. The person who passes, or shoves it, as it is called, having but one "piece" at a time. The fellow with the boodle keeps close in the wake of the shover, to receive the good money, and supply him with the counterfeit, as occasion requires.

BOOBY-HATCH Station-house; watch-house.

BOOKED Arrested.

BOOLY-DOG An officer; a policeman.

BOOZE Intoxicating drink.

BORDELLO A house of ill-fame.

BOSHING A flogging.

BOTTLE-HEAD A stupid fellow.

BOTS Boots.

BOUNCE To scold; blow up; to swagger; to convince by the force of sound more than sense.

BOUNCER A fellow that robs while bargaining with the store-keeper.

BOUNCING CHEAT A bottle.

BOUNG A purse.

BOWER A prison.

BOWSPRIT IN PARENTHESIS A pulled nose.

BRACKET-MUG A very ugly face.

BRADS Money.

BRAG To boast.

BRASS Money.

BREAD-BAG The stomach.

BREAKUPS Steamboat-landings; dispersing of people from theatres, lecture-rooms, churches, etc.

BREAK-O'-DAY DRUM A place for the sale of liquor, that never closes day or night.

BRIEF Duplicate.

BROADY Materials of any kind.

BROAD PITCHING The game of three-card monte.

BROADS Cards.

BROKEN LEG A woman that has had a child out of marriage.

BROTHER OF THE BLADE A soldier.

BROTHER OF THE BOLUS A doctor.

BROTHER OF THE BUSKIN An actor.

BROTHER OF THE BUNG A brewer.

BROTHER OF THE COIF A counsellor-at-law.

BROTHER OF THE GUSSET A pimp.

BROTHER OF THE QUILL An author; an editor.

BROTHER OF THE STRING Fiddler, or musician.

BROTHER OF THE SURPLICE A minister.

BROTHER OF THE WHIP A coachman.

BRUSH To flatter; to humbug; an encounter. "It was the hardest brush I ever saw; both men were as game as pebbles. It was noting but cut, carve, and come again."

BRUSHER A full glass.

BRUSHING UP A FLAT Praising or flattering.

BRUISER A fighter.

BUBB To drink; "Bubb your lush," drink your grog.

BUBBLE To cheat.

BUCK A hack-driver; bail.

BUCKET A live man.

BUCKLER A collar.

BUCKS-FACE A cuckold.

BUDGE A thief that sneaks into a store, and hides until the persons who lock up are gone, when he lets in his accomplice.

BUFE A dog.

BUFE-NAPPER A dog-thief; a mean rogue.

BUFFER A pugilist.

BUFFET A false swearer.

BUFFING IT HOME Swearing point blank to a circumstance or thing.

BUG A breast-pin.

BUGGING Taking money from a thief by a policeman.

BUGABOSE Sheriff's officers.

BUGAROCH Handsome; very pretty.

BUGGER A pickpocket; a buggsman.

BULL A locomotive.

BULL-DOGS Pistols.

BULL-TRAPS Rogues who personate officers for the purpose of extorting money.

BULLY A lump of lead tied in a corner of a kerchief.

BULLY TIMES Good times.

BULK AND FILE Shop-lifters; two pickpockets operating together — the "bulk" jostles the party that is to be robbed, and the "file" steals the treasure.

BUMMER A sponger.

BUMY-JUICE Porter or beer.

BUN A fellow that can not be shaken off.

BUNG A purse or pocket.

BURNING Cheating.

BURNERS Rogues who cheat countrymen with false cards or dice.

BURSTER A burglar. Sometimes it denotes bread.

BURNT OUT Worn-out roués; fellows that sorrow for the past, fear the future, and can only make the present endurable through means that are revolting to human reason.

BURST The conclusion of an entertainment; a spree.

BUSTLED Confused; perplexed; puzzled.

BUS-NAPPER A constable.

BUST To enter forcibly; a burglary.

BUTTEKER A store.

BUTTER-KEN A shop or store.

BUTTERED Whipped.

BUTTON To secure; to entice a simpleton to play.

BUZZING Searching for. "I was in a push and had to buzz about half a glass before I touched a flat's thimble and slang. I fenced the swag for half a century" — "I was in a crowd and searched for half an hour before I succeeded in stealing a man's watch and chain, which I sold for fifty dollars."

C

CAB-MOLL A woman that keeps a bad house.

CACKLE To blab. "The cove cackles" — tells all he knows.

CAD A baggage-smasher; a railroad conductor.

CADGER A beggar; a mean thief.

CADY A hat.

CAG Sulky; morose.

CAIN AND ABEL A table.

CAKE An easy fool of a policeman; a flat cop.

CALF-SKIN FIDDLE A drum.

CALLE A gown.

CAM Cambric, "Cam wiper." Cambric kerchief.

CAMESOR A shirt or shift.

CAN A dollar.

CANARY-BIRD A convict.

CANK Dumb.

CANT A gift; to give.

CANNIS COVE A dog-man; a dog-merchant; a dog-thief.

CAN'T SEE Very drunk; so that he can not see a hole through a ladder.

CAP To join in, "I will cap in with him" — I will appear to be his friend.

CAPPER One who supports another's assertion, to assist in cheating, "The burner bammed the flat with sham books, and his pal capped in for him" — The sharp cheated the countryman with false cards, and his confederate assisted (capped) in the fraud.

CAPER COVE A dancing-master.

CAP BUNG Hand it over; give it to me.

CAPTAIN HEEMAN A blustering fellow; a coward.

CAPTAIN TOPER A smart highwayman.

CAP YOUR LUCKY Run away.

CARAVAN Plenty of cash; rich; money enough.

CARLER A clerk.

CART OF TOGS A gift of clothes.

CARREL Jealous.

CASA A house, "Tout that casa" — mark that house. "It is all bob; let's dub the gig of the casa" — Now the coast is clear; let us break open the door of the house.

CASE A dollar.

CASS Cheese.

CASSE A house.

CAST Course, "He traversed the cast" — he walked the course.

CASTER A cloak.

CASTOR A hat.

CAT A drunken prostitute; a cross old woman; a muff; a pewter pot.

CATAMARAN An ugly woman.

CAT AND MOUSE Keeps house, "He keeps a cat and mouse."

CATCH-POLE A constable.

CATTER A crowbar.

CAVED Gave up; surrendered.

CAXON A wig.

CENTURY One hundred dollars; one hundred.

CHAFF Humbug.

CHAFER The treadmill.

CHAFFEY Boisterous; happy; jolly.

CHAFFING Talking; bantering.

CHALK To mark; to spot.

CHALKS To walk your chalks; to run away.

CHALK FARM The arm.

CHANT Talk; to publish; to inform. "Give me your chant," Give me your name.

CHARLEY A gold watch.

CHARM A picklock.

CHAPT Dry; thirsty.

CHATES Gallows.

CHANT COVES Reporters.

CHATTS Lice. Chatt, a louse.

CHATTY FEEDER A spoon.

CHARLEY PRESCOT A vest.

CHEESE Be silent; listen. "Cheese it, the coves are fly," be silent, the people understand us.

CHERRY PIPE A pipe; a full-grown woman.

CHIE Who is it? do you know?

CHIN A child.

CHINK Money.

CHINKERS Handcuffs and leg-irons united by a chain; money.

CHIPS Money.

CHIVE A file or saw. "Chive your darbies," file your irons off.

CHIVEY To scold.

CHOKER A neckerchief.

CHOVEY A shop or store.

CHOPPED UP When large quantities of goods are sold to a receiver, they are divided into small lots, and put into various houses, and this is called "chopping up the swag."

CHRISTENING Erasing the name of the maker from a stolen watch and putting another in its place.

CHURCH A term of endearment, "My church."

CHUMP Head.

CITY COLLEGE The Tombs.

CLANKERS Silver vessels.

CLARET Blood.

CLEAN Expert; smart.

CLEAR Run; go away; be off.

CLERKED Imposed upon. "The flat will not be clerked."

CLEYMANS Artificial sores made by beggars to impose on the credulous.

CLICK A blow; a thrust.

CLICKER A knock down.

CLINK To grab; to snatch; be quick; start.

CLOUT Handkerchief.

CLOWER A basket.

CLY A pocket.

CLY-FAKING Picking pockets.

COACHWHEEL A dollar.

COCKED HIS TOES UP Dead. "He is dead."

COCK AND HEN CLUB A place frequented by thieves of both sexes.

COCUM Sly; wary.

COFFEE Beans.

COG To cheat; to impose; a tooth.

COGLIONE A fool; a woman's dupe; a fop.

COLD DECK A prepared deck of cards played on a novice or "sucker."

COLD PIG A person that has been robbed of his clothes.

COLLAR To seize or take.

COLLARED Taken; arrested.

COLLEGE A State prison.

COLLEGE CHUM A fellow-prisoner.

COLTMAN One who lets horses and vehicles to burglars.

COMMISTER A parson.

COMMISSION A shirt or shift.

COMMIT To inform.

CONK The nose.

CONSOLATION Assassination. To
kill a man, is to give him consolation.
CONVENIENT A mistress.
CONFIDENCE MAN A fellow that
by means of extraordinary powers of
persuasion gains the confidence of his
victims to the extent of drawing upon
their treasury, almost to an unlimited
extent. To every knave born into the
world it has been said that there is a
due proportion of fools. Of all the
rogue tribe, the Confidence man is, perhaps, the most liberally supplied with
subjects; for every man has his soft
spot, and nine times out of ten the soft
spot is softened by an idiotic desire to
overreach the man that is about to over-
reach us. This is just the spot on which
the Confidence man works. He knows
his subject is only a knave wrongside
out, and accordingly he offers him a
pretended gold watch at the price of a
brass one; he calls at the front door
with presents from no where, as none
could be expected; he writes letters in
the most generous spirit, announcing
large legacies to persons who have no
kin on the face of the earth who cares a
copper for them. The Confidence man
is perfectly aware that he has to deal
with a man who expects a result without having worked for it, who gapes,
and stands ready to grasp at magnifi-

cent returns. The consequence is, that the victim — the confiding man — is always *done*. The one plays a sure game; his sagacity has taught him that the great study of the mass of mankind is to get something and give nothing; but as this is bad doctrine, he wakes up out of his "brown study," and finds himself, in lieu of his fine expectations, in possession of a turnip for a watch, a cigar-box in place of a casket. The Confidence man always carries the trump card; and whoever wishes to be victimized can secure his object by making a flat of himself in a small way, while attempting to victimize somebody else.

COPPED Arrested. "The knuck was copped to rights, a skin full of honey was found in his kick's poke by the copper when he frisked him," the pick-pocket was arrested, and when searched by the officer, a purse was found in his pantaloons pocket full of money.

COPPED TO RIGHTS Arrested on undoubted evidence of guilt.

COPBUSY The act of handing over stolen property by a thief to one of his pals for the purpose of preventing its being found on him if arrested.

COOK Melt; dissolve.

CORINTH A bad house.

CORINTHIANS Bad women who move in respectable society.

CORN-THRASHERS Farmers.

COUPLE To live with.

COVE OR COVEY A man.

COVER The fellow that covers the pickpocket while he is operating.

COVING Palming; stealing jewelry before the face and eyes of the owner, or person that is selling it.

COW A dilapidated prostitute.

COW'S GREASE Butter.

COW JUICE Milk.

COWS AND KISSES Miss, or the ladies.

CRACK To force; to burst open.

CRACKSMAN A burglar who uses force instead of picklocks or false keys.

CRABS Feet.

CRAB-SHELLS Shoes.

CRAMP WORDS Sentence of death.

CRAMPED Killed; murdered; hanged.

CRAMMER A falsehood.

CRAMP-RINGS Shackles or handcuffs.

CRANKY Mad; insane.

CRANKY-HUTCH An insane asylum.

CRAMPING CULL Executioner; hangman.

CRASH To kill. "Crash that cull," kill that fellow.

CREAMY Secretly.

CREATURE Liquor.

CREEME To slip money into the hands of another.

CRIB A house.

CROAKE To murder; to die.

CROAKED Dead.

CROAKERS Newspapers.

CROKUS A doctor. "The cove sold a stiff un to a crokus for twenty cases," the rogue sold a corpse to a doctor for twenty dollars.

CROSLEITE To cheat a friend.

CROSS Dishonest.

CROSS-COVE A thief; any person that lives in a dishonest way is said to be "on the cross," from the fact that highwaymen were in the habit of waiting for their victims on the cross-roads.

CROSS-DRUM A drinking-place where thieves resort.

CROSSED To meet another and pass him. "The swell moved as he crossed me," the gentleman bowed as he passed me.

CROSS-FANNING Picking a pocket with the arms folded across the chest. A knuck in the front rank of a crowd desiring to steal a watch from the pocket of a gentleman standing on either side of him, first folds his arms across his breast; and pretending to be intensely looking at some object before him, stretches out the arm next his victim, and by rapid movements of his fingers and hands excites his attention, and, while in this attitude, with the hand which is stretched across his own breast, he twists the watch from the other's pocket.

CROW The crow is the fellow that watches outside when his accomplices are inside, and gives them warning of the approach of danger.

CRUMEY Fat; pockets full; plenty.

CRUMP One who procures false witnesses.

CRUSHER A policeman.

CUES The points.

CUFFIR A man.

CUFFIN QUEERS Magistrates.

CULING Snatching reticules and purses from ladies.

CULL A man; sometimes a partner.

CUPSHOT Drunk.

CUPBOARD LOVE He or she loves only for what they can get.

CURLERS Fellows who sweat gold coins by putting them in a bag, and after violently shaking, gather the dust.

CURTISONS Broken-down lawyers; Tombs skinners.

CURBINGLAW Stealing goods out of windows.

CUSSINE A male.

CUT To abandon; to renounce acquaintance; drunk; "Half cut," half drunk.

CUT BENE Pleasant words; to speak kind.

CUTTER A peculiar instrument that first-class screwsmen (burglars) use for cutting through iron chests, doors, etc.

CUTTING HIS EYES Beginning to see; learning; suspicious.

CUTTY-EYED To look out of the corner of the eyes; to look suspicious; to leer; to look askance. "The copper cutty-eyed us," the officer looked suspicious at us.

CUT UP "The jug cut up very fat, and the gonniffs all got their regulars; there was no sinking in that mob," the bank was very rich, and the thieves all received their share; there was no cheating in that gang.

CYMBAL A watch.

D

DACE Two cents.

DADDLES Hands.

DAGAN A sword.

DAIRY The breasts of a woman that suckles a baby.

DAISY-ROOTS Boots and shoes.

DAISYVILLE The country.

DAKMA Silence; "Dakma the bloke, and cloy his cole," silence the man, and steal his money.

DAMBER First.

DAMBER COVE The head man.

DANAN Stairs.

DANCE AT HIS DEATH To be hung; "May he dance when he dies," may he be hanged.

DANCERS Shooting stars; fellows who do not remain long in one place.

DANCING Sneaking up stairs to commit a larceny.

DANGLER A roué; a seducer.

DANGLERS A bunch of seals.

DAPPER Well made. "The crack was dapper."

DARBIES Handcuffs; fetters.

DARBY Cash. "Fork over the darby," hand over the cash.

DARK CULLEY A man who visits his mistress only at night.

DARKEY A dark lantern. "The coves had screwed the gig of the jug, when Jack flashed the darkey into it, and found it planted full of coppers. 'Bingavast!' was the word; some one has cackled," the thieves had opened the door of a bank with false keys, and when they looked in with the aid of a dark lantern, they found the place filled with officers. One of the thieves cried out: "Be off! some one has cackled."

DAUB A ribbon.

DAVEY Affidavit; to witness under oath.

DAWB To bribe. "The bene cove was scragged, because he could not dawb the beak," the good fellow was hanged, because he could not bribe the judge.

DAY-LIGHTS The eyes.

DEAD BROKE Not a cent.

DEAD BEAT Without hope; certain.

DEAD GAME A term used by gamblers when they have a certainty of winning.

DEAD TO RIGHTS Positively guilty, and no way of getting clear.

DEAD SET A concentrated attack on a person or thing.

DEAD SWAG Not worth so much as it was thought to be; things stolen that are not easily disposed of.

DEATH HUNTER The undertaker.

DEEK THE COVE See the fellow; look at him.

DELLS A prostitute.

DERREY An eye-glass.

DEVIL BOOKS Cards.

DEW-BEATERS The feet.

DEWS A gold eagle; ten dollars.

DIAL-PLATE The face.

DIARY To remember; to enter in a book. "I'll diary the joskin," I'll remember the fool.

DIB Portion or share.

DIBS Money.

DIDDLE Liquor.

DIDDLE COVE A landlord.

DIE Dummy, or pocket-book.

DIFT COVE A neat little man.

DIGGERS Finger-nails.

DIMBER Handsome; pretty.

DIMBER-MORT Pretty girl; enchanting girl.

DING To throw away; to strike.

D.I.O. Damn it! I'm off.

DIP A kiss in the dark; a pickpocket.

DIP To pick a pocket; the act of putting a hand into a pocket.

DIPT Pawned.

DISMAL DITTY The psalm or hymn sung by persons just before they are hanged.

DISPATCH A mittimus; a warrant of arrest.

DIVER A pickpocket.

DIVING Picking pockets.

DIVING-BELL A rum-shop in a basement.

DOASH A cloak.

DOBING LAY To steal from stores early in the morning. Two thieves enter a store, as soon as the porter opens it; one of them inquires about some goods he pretends he was looking at the day before, and wishes to see them. The goods inquired for are either in the back of the store or upstairs. In the absence of the porter, the other fellow robs the store.

DOCTORS False cards or dice.

DOCTOR GREEN A young inexperienced fellow.

DOG-NIPPERS Rogues who steal dogs, and restore them to their owners after a reward has been offered.

DOGS-PASTE Sausage-meat; mince-meat.

DOING POLLY Picking oakum in prison.

DOLLY SHOP A loan office.

DOMESTIC Made at home. The man robbed himself; some one in the house assisted the thieves. "You may look at home for the thief."

DOMMERER A fellow that pretends to be deaf and dumb.

DONE Convicted.

DONKEY-RIDING Cheating in weight or measure; miscounting.

DONNEZ To give.

DOPEY A thief's mistress.

DOOKIN COVE A fortune-teller.

DOSE Burglary.

DOSS A bed. "The badger got under the doss, and frisked the bloke's pokes of two centuries and a half, and then bounced the flat till he mizzled."

DOTS Money.

DOWN Hatred; dislike; vindictive; to suspect another. "The copper cutty-eyed me and measured my mug, and is down on the job," the officer looked at me from the corners of his eyes, and examined my face; he suspects what we are about.

DOWNEY A smooth, pleasant talker; a knowing fellow.

DOWNER A five cent piece.

DOWSE To strike. "Dowse his mug." hit is face.

DONBITE A street.

DOXIE A girl.

DRAB A nasty woman.

DRAG A cart or wagon.

DRAGGING Stealing from shop-
doors.
DRAGONS Sovereigns; gold coins.
DRAGSMAN A thief that steals from
express wagons and carts; also trunks
from the back of coaches. They sometimes have a fast horse and light wagon.
DRAY Three.

DRAW

DRAWING
} Picking pockets.
"I say, my
kinchin, what's
your lay?" "Vy,
yer see, as how I
am learning to
draw."

DROMEDARY A clumsy, blundering
fellow.
DROPS, or DROPPERS Fellows that
cheat country-men by dropping a
pocket-book filled with bad money,
near their heels, and then pretend that
they found it. By the aid of an accomplice, the countryman is induced to purchase it, with the avowed intention of
finding the real owner, believing it to
contain good money.
DROPT DOWN Low-spirited. "The
kiddy dropt down when he went to be
scragged," the youngster was very low-
spirited when he walked out to be
hanged.
DRUM A drinking-place.

DRUMSTICK A club.

DRY UP Be silent; stop that.

DUB Lay Robbing houses by picking the locks.

DUB A key; a picklock.

DUCE Two cents; two.

DUB O' THE HICK A blow on the head. The copper tipt the dromedary a dub o' the hick with his drum-stick.

DUB THE JIGGER Open the door.

DUBLER A picker of locks.

DUDS Clothes.

DUFF Pudding.

DUFFER A fellow, in the dress of a sailor, who knocks at the basement-door, and inquires if the lady of the house does not want to buy some smuggled goods, and then exhibits imitation silks, satins, Irish linens, etc., etc., which he pretends to have run ashore without the knowledge of the custom-house officers.

DUKES The hands.

DUMMY A pocket-book; a portmonnaie. "Frisk the dummy of the screens, ding it and bolt; they are crying out beef," take out the money and throw the pocket-book away; run, they are crying, stop thief!

DUN A *very importunate* creditor. Dunny, in the provincial dialect of several counties in England, signifies *deaf;* to dun, then, perhaps may mean to deafen with *importunate demands*; it may have been derived from the word *donnez,* which signifies give. But the word undoubtedly originated in the days of one Joe Dun, a famous bailiff of the town of Lincoln, England, who was so extremely active and dexterous in his business, that it became a proverb, when a man refused to pay, to say, "Why don't you Dun him?" that is, send Dun after him. Hence it became a cant word, and is now as old as the days of Henry VII. Dun was also the name for the hangman, before that of Jack Ketch.

"And presently a halter got,
Made of the best strong hempen teer,
And ere a cat could lick her ear,
Had tied it up with as much art,
As Dun himself could do for's
heart."
Cotton's Virgil Trav. Book IV.

DUNNAKIN It can't be helped; necessary.
DUNNOCK A cow.
DUNEKER A thief that steals cattle.
DUNNEY Deaf; to dun.
DURIA Fire.
DUSTMAN Dead man. "Poor Bill is a dustman; he was a bene cove," poor Bill is dead; he was a good man.

DUSTY Dangerous. "Two fly-cops and a beak tumbled to us, and Bill thought as how it was rather dusty, and so, shady was the word," two detectives and a magistrate came upon us suddenly; Bill said it was rather dangerous, and so we got out of sight.

E

EARTH-BATH A grave.

EASE To rob.

EASE THE COVE Rob the man.

EASON To tell.

EASY Killed. "Make the cull easy," kill him; gag him.

EAT To take back; to recall; to retract; to unsay.

EAVES A hen-roost; a poultry house.

EAVESDROPPER A mean fellow; a petty larceny vagabond.

EDGE Encourage; persuade; induce.

EGROTAT He is sick.

ELBOW Turn the corner; get out of sight.

ELBOW-SHAKER A man that gambles with dice.

ELEPHANT The fellow has an enormous booty, and knows not how to secrete it. If he had less, he would be able to save more.

ELFEN Walk light; on tiptoe.

EMPEROR A drunken man.

ENGLISH BURGUNDY London porter.

EQUIPT Rich; full of money; well dressed, "The cull equipped me with a deuce of finifs," the man gave me two five-dollar bills.

ERIFFS Young thieves; minor rogues.

ETERNITY-BOX A coffin.

EVERLASTING The treadmill.

EVIL A wife; a halter; matrimony.

EWE An old woman dressed like a young girl, "An old ewe dressed lamb fashion." "A white ewe," a beautiful woman.

EXECUTION-DAY Wash-day; cleaning house.

EYE Nonsense; humbug.

F

FACER A glass filled so full that there is no room for the lip; a staller, or one who places himself in the way of persons who are in hot pursuit of his accomplices.

FADGE It won't do, "It won't fadge."

FAG A lawyer's clerk; to beat. "Fag the flat," beat the fool.

FAGGER A small boy put into a window to rob the house, or to open it for others to rob.

FAGGOT To bind. "Faggot the culls," bind the men.

FAIKING Cutting out the wards of a key.

FAITHFUL A tailor that gives long credit. "I say, Sam, what kind of crib was that you cracked?" "Oh! it belonged to one of the faithful."

FAKEMENT A written or printed paper; the written deposition of a witness.

FAKER A jeweller.

FAM GRASP To shake hands. "Fam grasp the cove," shake hands with the fellow.

FAMILY-MAN A receiver of stolen goods from a dwelling-house.

FAMLY-MAN Connected with thieves.

FAM LAY Thieves who rob jewellers' stores by pretending to want to make a purchase.

FAMS Hands.

FAN A waistcoat.

FANNY BLAIR The hair.

FARMER An alderman.

FASTNER A warrant.

FAT Money.

FATERS Fortune-tellers.

FEEDERS Silver spoons or forks. "Nap the feeders," steal the spoons.

FEKER Trade; profession.

FEINT A pawn-broker.

FEN A common woman.

FENCE A receiver of stolen goods; to sell stolen goods. "The bloke fenced the swag for five cases," the fellow sold the plunder for five dollars.

FENCED Sold.

FERM A hole.

FIB To beat. "Fib the bloke's quarron in the rumpad, and draw the honey in his poke," beat the fellow's carcase in the street, and steal the money in his pocket.

FIBBING Striking with the fist.

FIDLAM BENS Thieves who have no particular lay, whose every finger is a fish-hook; fellows that will steal any thing they can remove.

FIDLAM COVES Small thieves who steal any thing they can lay hands on.

FIGDEAN To kill.

FIGGER A juvenile thief put through side-lights at outside doors to unbolt the door and admit other thieves to the house.

FIGNER A small thief.

FIGGING LAW The art of picking pockets.

FIGURE-DANCER One who alters the numbers or figures on bank-bills.

FILE A pick-pocket. The file is one who is generally accompanied by two others, one of whom is called the "Adam tyler;" and the other the "bulker," or "staller." It is their business to jostle, or "ramp" the victim, while the "file" picks his pocket and then hands the plunder to the Adam tyler, who makes off with it.

FINE Imprisoned. "The cove had a fine of two stretchers and a half imposed upon him for relieving a joskin of a load of cole," the fellow was sentenced to imprisonment for stealing a countryman's money.

FINGER-BETTER A fellow who wants to bet on credit, and indicates the favorite card by pointing to it with his finger.

FINNIFF Five dollars.

FIRE Danger. "This place is all on fire; I must pad like a bull or the cops will nail me," every body is after me in this place; I must run like a locomotive or the officers will arrest me.

FISH A seaman.

FITTER A fellow that fits keys to locks for burglars.

FIZZLE To escape. "The cove made a fizzle," the fellow escaped.

FIZZLED Broke up; fell through.

FLAG ABOUT A low strumpet.

FLAM To humbug. "Flam the bloke," humbug the fellow.

FLAME A mistress.

FLAPPERS Hands.

FLASH Knowing; to understand another's meaning; to "patter flash," to speak knowingly.

FLASH-DRUM A drinking-place resorted to by thieves.

FLASH-HOUSE A house of resort for thieves.

FLASH-KEN A thieves' boarding-house.

FLASH-MAN A fellow that has no visible means of living, yet goes dressed in fine clothes, exhibiting a profusion of jewelry about his person.

FLASH YOUR IVORY Laugh; show your teeth.

FLASH HER DILES Spend her money.

FLASH PANNY A house resorted to by rogues of both sexes.

FLAT A man that is not acquainted with the tricks and devices of rogues.

FLATTER-TRAP The mouth.

FLAWED Half-drunk; quick-tempered; not exactly honest.

FLAY To vomit.

FLESH-BROKER A match maker; a procuress.

FLICKER To drink. "Flicker with me," drink with me.

FLICKERING Laughing; smiling; drinking.

FLICKING Cutting. "Flick me some panam and caffar," cut me some bread and cheese. "Flick the Peter and rake the swag, for I want to pad my beaters," cut the portmanteau and divide the plunder. I want to walk my boots, (to be off.)

FLIMP To tussle; to wrestle.

FLIMPING Garroting; highway robbery.

FLIMSEY A bank-note.

FLING To get the best of another. "The sharp will fling the bloke," the rogue will cheat the man.

FLOORERS or TRIPPERS Fellows that cause persons to slip or fall in the street, and then, while assisting them up, steal their watch or portmonnaie. They are sometimes called "rampers."

A gentleman in a hurry on his way to the bank, or any other place of business, is suddenly stopped by a fellow directly in front of him, going in an opposite direction to himself, who has apparently slipped or stumbled, and in endeavoring to save himself from falling, thrusts his head into the pit of the gentleman's stomach, thereby knocking him down. Immediately two very kind gentlemen, one on each side, assist him to rise, and when on his feet busy themselves in brushing the dirt from his clothing, during which operation they pick his pockets. Thanking his kind assistants with much profuseness, he goes on his way, and very soon afterwards finds himself minus his watch or pocket-book, and perhaps both.

FLUE-SCRAPERS Chimney-sweeps.

FLUSH Plenty; the cove.

FLUTE The recorder of a city.

FLUX To cheat; cozen; over-reach.

FLY Knowing; up to him. "The bloke was fly, and I could not draw his fogle," the man was aware of what I wanted, and I could not steal his handkerchief.

FLY-COP Sharp officer; an officer that is well posted; one who understands his business.

FLYERS Shoes.

FLYING COVES Fellows who obtain money by pretending to persons who have been robbed, that they can give them information that will be the means of recovering their lost goods.

FLYING JIGGERS Turnpike-gates.

FOB To cheat.

FOG Smoke.

FOGLE A pocket-handkerchief.

FOGLE-HUNTING Stealing pocket-handkerchiefs.

FOGRAM A fusty old fellow.

FOGUE Fierce; fiery; impetuous.

FOGUS Tobacco. "Tip me a gage of fogus," give me a cigar, or a pipe and tobacco.

FORK A pickpocket.

FORKS The fore and middle fingers.

FOXEY Cunning; crafty; sly.

FOXING To pretend to be asleep.

FOYST A cheat.

FOYSTER A pickpocket.

FRAMER A shawl.

FREE To steal.

FRENCH CREAM Brandy — called "French cream," by the old Tabbies, when mixed with their tea.

FRIDAY Hangman's day.

FRIDAY FACE A dismal countenance; the face of a man who is sentenced to be executed.

FRISK To search; to examine.

FROG A policeman.

FROG AND TOE The city of New-York. "Coves, let us frog and toe," coves, let us go to New-York.

FRUMPER A sturdy blade.

FUBSEY Plump.

FUBSEY DUMMEY A fat pocket-book.

FULLIED Committed for trial.

FUMBLES Gloves.

FUN To cheat. "To fun a man," is to cheat him.

FUNK To frighten.

FUNKED OUT Frightened; backed out.

FUNKERS The very lowest order of thieves.

FUSSOCK And old fat woman.

FUSTIAN Wine.

G

GABS Talk.

GABBEY A foolish fellow.

GADDING THE HOOF Going without shoes.

GAFF A theatre; a fair. "The drop-coves maced the joskins at the gaff," the ring-droppers cheated the countrymen at the fair.

GAFFING Tossing; pitching; throwing.

GAGE Man; fellow. "Deck the gage," see the man.

GAGERS Eyes.

GAIT Manner; fashion; way; profession. "I say, Tim, what's your gait now?" "Why, you see, I'm on the crack," (burglary.).

GALENA Salt pork.

GALIGASKIN A pair of breeches.

GAM Stealing.

GAME The particular line of rascality the rogue is engaged in; thieving; cheating.

GAMMON To deceive. "What rum gammon the old sharp pitched into the flat," how finely the knowing old fellow flattered the fool.

GAMMY Bad.

GAN The mouth or lips.

GANDER A married man not living at home with his wife.

GANG Company; squad; mob.

GAPESEED Wonderful stories; any thing that will cause people to stop, look, or listen.

GARRET The head.

GARRETTING To rob a house by entering it through the scuttle or an upper window.

GARROTE To choke.

GARROTERS Fellows that rob by choking their victim. Three fellows work together in this manner: The tallest of the three steps behind the victim, and putting his right arm around the neck, compresses the windpipe, and at the same time, locks the right leg by throwing his own around it. Another of the confederates secures his hands, while the third rifles his pockets. Should the garroting be done on a public thoroughfare, where people are passing, the garroters engage in laughter and jocular remarks, as if it were a pleasant lark among friends. They sometimes sprinkle rum on and about the victim's neck and face, so as to induce persons who find him, after they have left him half-dead and stupified, to believe that he is drunk.

GATTER Drink of any kind.

GELTER Money.

GERMAN FLUTE A pair of boots.

GETAWAY A locomotive; railroad train.

GHOULS Fellows who watch assignation-houses, and follow females that come out of them to their homes and then threaten to expose them to their husbands, relatives, or friends, if they refuse to give them not only money, but also the use of their bodies.

GIG A door. "Dub the gig of the casa," break open the door of the house.

GIGG A nose. "Snitchel the bloke's gigg," smash the man's nose.

GIGGER A lock or door. "Dub the gigger," open the door.

GIGGER-DUBBER A turn-key; a prison-keeper.

GIG-LAMPS A pair of spectacles.

GILFLIRT A proud, capricious woman.

GILL A woman.

GILT or JILT A crowbar.

GILT-DUBBER A hotel thief.

GILYORE Plenty.

GINGERLY Cautiously.

GIP A thief.

GLASS An hour. "The badger piped his Moll about a glass and a half before she cribbed the flat."

GLAZE Break the glass. "I say, Bill, you mill the glaze, and I'll touch the swag and mizzle," I say, Bill, you break the glass, and I will steal the goods and run away.

GLAZIER A fellow that breaks windows or showcases, to steal the goods exposed for sale.

GLIB Smooth; polite. "The bloke is glib," the fellow is polite.

GLIBE Writing; a written agreement.

GLIMS Eyes.

GLIMSTICKS Candlesticks.

GLIM Flashy In a passion; savage.

GLIMMER The fire.

GLUM Sombre; low-spirited.

GLUTTON A fellow that can stand a great deal of beating.

GNOSTICS Knowing ones; smart fellows; sharps.

GNARLER A little dog, who, by his barking, alarms the family. Gnarlers are more feared by burglars than guns or pistols.

GOAWAYS Railroad trains. "The knuck was working the goaways at Jersey City, and had but just touched a bloke's leather, as the bull bellowed for the last time, and so the cove mizzled through the jigger. The flat roared beef; but it was no go, as the bull was going very mad," the pickpocket was busy in the cars at Jersey City, and had

58

just stolen a man's pocket-book, as the locomotive blew its whistle for the last time. The thief bolted through the door, and off the cars, just as the victim had discovered his loss and cried, "stop thief!" But it was of no avail, as the locomotive was going very fast.

GO The fashion. "All the go," all the fashion.

GOADS Peter Funks; cappers in.

GO BACK To turn against. "He won't go back on the cove; he is staunch," he will not turn against the fellow, for he is a true man.

GOATER Dress.

GOB The mouth.

GOBSTICKS Silver forks or spoons.

GOBSTRING A bridle.

GODFATHERS Jurymen; so called because they name the degrees of crime as to grand or petit larceny, etc, etc.

GOLDFINCH Gold coin.

GONNOFF A thief that has attained the higher walks of his profession.

GOOH A prostitute.

GOREE Gold dust.

GORGER A gentleman; a well-dressed man.

GOOSECAP A silly fellow; a fool.

GOOSEBERRY-LAY Stealing wet clothes from clothes-lines or bushes.

GOOSEBERRY-PUDDING Woman.

GOOSING SLUM A brothel.

GOT HIM DOWN CLOSE Know all about him; know where to find him.

GOT HIM DOWN FINE Know for a certainty; Know all his antecedents.

GO THE JUMP Sneak into a room through the window.

GOVERNOR'S STIFF A governor's pardon.

GRABBED Arrested.

GRABBLE To seize. "You grabble the goose-cap and I'll frisk his pokes," you seize the fool, and I'll search his pockets.

GRAFT To work.

GRAFTING Working; helping another to steal.

GRASSVILLE The country.

GREASE A bribe. "Grease the copper in the fist, and he'll be as blind as your mother," put money in the officer's hand, and he will not watch you.

GREED Money.

GRIG A merry fellow.

GRIM Death; "Old Grim."

GRIN A skeleton.

GRIPE-FIST A broker; a miser.

GROANERS Thieves who attend at charity sermons, and rob the congregation of their watches and purses, exchange bad hats for good ones, steal the prayer-books, etc., etc.

GROGHAM A horse.

GROPERS Blind men.

GROUND SWEAT A grave.

GRUEL Coffee.

GRUNTER A country constable.

GUMMEY-STUFF Medicine.

GUN To watch; to examine; to look at.

GUN A thief.

GUNNED Looked at; examined. "The copper gunned me as if he was fly to my mug," the officer looked at me as if he knew my face.

GUNPOWDER A scolding or quick-tempered woman.

GUNS Pickpockets.

GUERRILLAS This name is applied by gamblers to fellows who skin suckers when and where they can, who do not like the professional gamblers, but try to beat them, sometimes inform on them, and tell the suckers that they have been cheated.

GUTTER Porter.

GUTTER-LANE The throat.

GUY A dark lantern.

H

HACKUM A bravado; a slasher. "Capt. Hackum," a fellow who slashes with a bowie-knife.

HALF-A-HOG A five-cent piece.

HALF-A-NED A five-dollar gold piece.

HALF-A-STRETCH Six months' imprisonment.

HAMLET A captain of police.

HAMS Pants.

HANDLE Nose. "The cove flashed a rare handle to his physog." The fellow has a very large nose.

HANG BLUFF Snuff.

HANG IT UP Think of it; remember it.

HANG OUT The place one lives in. "The cops scavey where we hang out," the officers know where we live.

HANGMAN'S DAY Friday is so called from the custom of hanging people on a Friday.

HANK To know something about a man that is disreputable. "He has a hank on the bloke whereby he sucks honey when he chooses," he knows something about the man, and therefore induces him to give him money when he chooses.

HARD Metal.

HARD COLE Silver or gold money.

HARDWARE False coin.

HARE IT Return; come back.

HARMAN A constable.

HARMAN BEAK The sheriff.

HARP A woman.

HARRIDAN A haggard old woman; a scold.

HASH To vomit.

HATCHES In distress; in trouble; in debt.

HAWK A confidence man; a swindler.

HAVIL A sheep.

HAVEY CAVEY Wavering; doubtful.

HEAVE To rob. "To heave a crib," to rob a house.

HEAVER The breast or chest of a person.

HEAVERS Persons in love.

HEAVING Stealing; taking. "The cove was done for heaving a peter from a cart," the fellow was convicted for stealing a trunk from a cart.

HEDGE To bet on both sides; to be friends with both sides; to pray "Good God," "Good Devil."

HEELS To run away.

HEELER An accomplice of the pocket-book dropper. The heeler stoops behind the victim, and strikes one of his heels as if by mistake; this draws his attention to the pocket-book that lies on the ground.

HEMP To choke.

HEMP THE FLAT Choke the fool.

HEN A woman.

HERRING All bad; all alike.

HICKEY Tipsy; not quite drunk; elated.

HICKJOP A fool.

HICKSAM A countryman; a fool.

HIGH BEAK The first judge; the president; the governor; the head official.

HIGHFLYER An audacious, lewd woman.

HIGH BLOKE A well-dressed fellow.

HIGH GAG Telling secrets; a fellow that whispers.

HIGH JINKS Small gamblers.

HIGH-LIVER A fellow who lives in a garret.

HIGH PADS Highway robbers.

HIGH ROPES In a passion; very loud.

HIGH TIDE Plenty of money.

HIGH TOBERS Gonnoffs; the highest order of thieves, who generally go well dressed, and frequent watering-places, etc., etc.

HIGH TOBY A highway robber.

HIKE Run away. "Hike; the cops have tumbled to us," run; the officers have seen us.

HIP INSIDE Inside coat-pocket.

HIP OUTSIDE Outside coat-pocket.

HISTORY OF THE FOUR KINGS A pack of cards. "The bloke's skin is lathy, he studies the history of the four kings closer than the autum-bawler's patter," the man's purse is thin; he studies a pack of cards more than the parson's sermons.

HOCK Caught in hock; caught by the heels. "If the cove should be caught in the hock he won't snickle," if the fellow should be caught in the act, he would not tell.

HOCKEY Drunk.

HOCKS The feet.

HOCUS To stupify. "Hocus the bloke's lush, and then frisk his sacks," put something into the fellow's drink that will stupify him, and then search his pockets.

HOBB A country-fellow.

HOBINOL A clown.

HOBNAIL A countryman.

HOB OR NOB What will you drink?

HOD A mason; a builder.

HOG IN ARMOR A blustering office-holder.

HOG IN TOGS A well-dressed loafer.

HOGO High-flavored; strong-scented.

HOGG A ten-cent piece.

HOGGING To humbug.

HOIST To rob houses by climbing into a window. It is generally done by two or three fellows, one of whom stands close to the house, and the others climb up on him to the window.

HOISTER A shop-lifter.

HOISTING Putting a man upright on his head, and shaking him until his money and watch fall out of his pockets; they hold this to be no robbery.

HOISTLAY *See Hoist.*

HOLLOW Certain; a decided beat.

HONEY Money.

HOODY-DOODY A short clump of a person.

HOOF Foot. "To beat the hoof," to travel on foot.

HOOKED To steal.

HOOKER A thief.

HOOP A ring.

HOOP IT Run away.

HOP THE TWIG Be off; go off.

HOPPED THE TWIG Hung.

HORNESS Watchman.

HORSE-CAPPERS Fellows that cheat simple people out of their money by the aid of a broken-down first-class horse.

HOSTEL A tavern.

HOT Too well known. "The cove had better move his beaters into Dewsville, it is too hot for him here; if he stops, he'll be sure to be sick for twenty stretches," the fellow had better go into the country, for if he stays, he will be sent to prison for twenty years.

HOUSE TO LET A widow's weeds.

HUBBUB Pain in the stomach.

HUE Lash him.

HUEY The National Police Gazette.

HUFF A bullying, cowardly fellow.

HUG To choke.

HUGGING THE HOOKER Choking the thief.

HUMBOX An auctioneer's rostrum.

HUMMER A great lie.

HUMPHREY A coat used by pickpockets, that has pocket-holes, but no pockets.

HUSH Murder. "Hush the bloke," kill the fellow.

HUSH-STUFF Money given to prevent a witness from testifying.

I

ICKEN Oak.

ICKEN BAUM An oak-tree.

IDEA-POT A man's head.

IMPOST-TAKER One who lends
money to thieves and gamblers at very
high rates.

IMPUDENT To cut the tails of a
man's coat.

IMPURE A lady of easy virtue.

INDORSER One who flogs another
on the back.

INGLERS Horse-dealers who cheat
those that deal with them.

INKLE Let him know.

INLAID Plenty of money saved.

INNOCENT A corpse.

INNOCENTS Convicts, because it is
supposed that they can not commit
crime.

INSIDER One who knows.

INTIMATE A shirt. "Intimate as your
shirt."

IRON Courage; fearless; staunch.

IRON DOUBLET Innocence; not
guilty.

IRONED Handcuffed.

IVY BUSH A very small-faced man who has a large quantity of hair on his face and head.

IVORIES The teeth. "How the blowen flashes her ivories," how the girl shows her teeth.

J

JABBER To talk in an unknown language.

JACK A small coin.

JACK COVE A mean low fellow.

JACK DANDY A little impertinent fellow.

JACKED Lamed.

JACKET To show one up; point one out. The fly cops pulled him, and allowed the flat cops to jacket him; so you see it was dusty for him, and I advised him to pike into Daisyville for a few moons until the down blew off.

JACK-GAGGER A fellow that lives on the prostitution of his wife.

JACK-KETCH The hangman. This cognomen for the hangman is of very ancient date. In the year 1682, we find in "Butler's Ghost," p. 54, the following lines:

"Till Ketch observing he was choused,
And in his province much abused;
In open hall the tribute dunned,
To do his office, or refund."

Jack Ketch had not been long appointed to his office; for we find the name of his predecessor (Dun) in the former part of this poem,

"For you, yourself, to act Squire
Dun,
Such ignominy ne'er saw the sun."

The addition of "Squire" to Dun's name was an evidence that he had executed some state criminal, which, according to the custom of the times, accorded to him that title. The predecessor of Dun was one Gregory; from whom the gallows was called the "Gregorian tree," and by which name it is mentioned in the prologue to "Mercurius Pragmaticus," tragi-comedy, acted in 1641:

"This trembles under the black rod,
and he
Doth fear his fate from the Gregorian tree."

Gregory succeeded Derrick, who flourished in the year 1608, as we find in an old book of that time: "For he rides his circuit with the devil, and Derrick must be his host, and Tyburn the inne at which he will light." "At the gallows where I leave them, as to the haven at which they must all cast anchor, if Derrick's cables do but hold."

JACOB A ladder.

JACOBITE A shirt-collar.

JACK OF LEGS A very tall fellow.

JACK-RUN A license.

JACK SPRAT A small fellow.

JACK WRIGHT A fat fellow.

JADE A long term of imprisonment.

JAGGER A gentleman.

JAGUE A cut; a ditch.

JAM A gold ring.

JAMMED Killed; murdered; hanged.

JANASMUG A go-between; one who goes between the thief and the fence.

JANAZARIES A mob of pickpockets.

JAPANNED A convict is said to be japanned when the chaplain pronounces him to be converted.

JARK A seal.

JARKMAN One who writes characters for servants, begging petitions, etc., etc.

JARVEY A driver.

JASKER A seal.

JAW COVES Auctioneers, lawyers.

JAZEY A man with an enormous quantity of hair on his head and face.

JEFFEY Lightning.

JEM A gold ring.

JENNEY A hook on the end of a stick.

JENNY LINDA A window, pronounced *winder*.

72

JERRY A chamber-pot.

JERRY-SNEAK A hen-pecked husband.

JESSANY A man well dressed.

JET AUTUM A parson.

JEW'S EYE A pleasant, agreeable sight.

JIG A trick.

JIGGER A door. "Dub the jigger," open the door.

JILT A prostitute who hugs and kisses a countryman while her accomplice robs him.

JILTER A sneak-thief.

JINGLEBRAINS A wild, thoughtless fellow.

JOB A robbery. "To do a job," to commit a robbery.

JOB Patience; take time; don't be in a hurry.

JOBATION A reproof; painful.

JOBBER-NOT A tall, ungainly fellow.

JOB'S DOCK An hospital. "The poor cove is in Job's dock," the poor fellow is in the hospital.

JOCK Enjoy; to enjoy any thing.

JOCKUM GAGE A chamber-pot.

JOEY A hypocrite. Sometimes, four.

JOLLY The head; an excuse; a pretense.

JOMER A mistress.

JORDAN Disagreeable; hard to be done.

JORDAIN A blow. "I'll tip the Jack
Cove a jordain on the jazey, if I
transnear him," I'll hit the mean fellow
with my club on his big nose, if I get
near him.

JOSEPH A coat that's patched; a
sheepish, bashful fellow.

JOSEPH'S COAT Guarded against
temptation. "I say, my bene blowen,
can't you kiddy the bloke?" "No,
Dick, it's of no use trying, he wears a
Joseph's coat," I say, my good girl,
can't you seduce the man? No, Dick,
its no use trying, he is guarded against
temptation.

JOSKIN A countryman; a silly fellow.
"The cove maced the joskin of twenty
cases,' the fellow cheated the countryman out of twenty dollars.

JUG A bank.

JUMP A widow; run away.

JUMPED HIS BAIL Run away from
his bail.

JUMPERS Fellows that rob houses by
getting into windows.

JURK A seal.

K

KATE A smart, brazen-faced woman.
KATEY A picklock.
KEELER A small tub, or firkin.
KEFFEL A horse.
KELTER Condition; order.
KE-KEYA Devil; Satan.
KEN A house. "Bite the ken," rob the house.
KEN-CRACKER A house-breaker.
KETCH Hang. "I'll ketch you," I'll hang you.
KICK A pocket. "The Moll stubbled her skin in her kick," the woman held her purse in her pocket.
KICK-CLOY A pair of breeches.
KICKSIES P ants; breeches.
KICKED THE BUCKET Dead.
KID A child; a youth; a young one.
KIDDED Coaxed; amused; humbugged. "The sneaksman kidded the cove of the crib, while his pal tapped the till," the thief amused the storekeeper, while his comrade robbed the money-drawer.
KIDDIES Young thieves.
KIDDEN A boy lodging-house.
KIDMENT Comical.

KIDSMAN A fellow that boards and lodges boys for the purpose of teaching them how to steal, putting them through a course of training, as a dog-trainer will train dogs for the hunt. The kidsman accompanies the kid, and though committing no depredations himself, he controls and directs the motions of the others.

KIDNEY The same kind.

KILL DEVIL New rum.

KIMBAW To bully; to beat. "Let's kimbaw the bloke," let us bully or beat the fellow.

KINCHIN A young child.

KINCHIN COVES Boys taught how to steal.

KINCHIN MORTS Girls educated to steal.

KIP A bed; half a fool.

KIRJALIS Who fears? I fear not; come on.

KIRKBUZZER A fellow that picks pockets in churches.

KIT A dancing-master; the implements of a burglar.

KITE A letter; fancy stocks.

KITCHEN PHYSIC Food. "A little kitchen physic will set me up." I have more need of a cook than a doctor.

KITING Restless; going from place to place.

KITTLE To tickle; to please.

KITTLER One who tickles or pleases.

KITTYS Stock in trade; tools. "The bobbies seized the screwsman's kittys," the officers seized the burglar's tools.

KLEM To strike. "Klem the bloke," hit the man.

KNAPPED Arrested.

KNIGHT OF ALSATIA A person that treats the whole company.

KNIGHT OF THE POST A fellow that will swear any thing for money.

KNOB The head.

KNOB-THATCHER A wig-maker.

KNOCK-ME-DOWN Very strong liquor.

KNOSE Tobacco; smoke.

KNOT A gang of thieves.

KNOWLEDGE-BOX The head.

KNUCK A pickpocket.

KONE Counterfeit money.

KONIACKER A counterfeiter.

L

LACE To beat; to whip.

LACED MUTTON A common woman.

LACH Let in. "The cove is bene, shall we lach him?" the man is good, shall we let him in? "If he is not leaky." "I'll answer for him; he is staunch."

LADDER "He mounted the ladder," he was hung.

LADY A humpbacked female.

LADY BIRD A kept mistress.

LAG A convicted felon.

LAGGED Convicted; transported.

LAGE Water; a basket.

LAGE OF DUDS A basket of clothes.

LAID Pawned.

LAMB To flog.

LAMBASTE Flog. "Lambaste the bloke," flog the fellow.

LAMBO To beat with a club.

LAMP Eye. "The cove has a queer lamp," the man has a blind or squinting eye.

LAND-YARD The grave-yard.

LAND-BROKER An undertaker. "The cove buys lands for stiff uns," the man purchases land for dead people.

LANTERN-JAWED Thin-faced.

LAP Drink; butter milk; pick it up; to take; to steal.

LAP UP To wipe out; to put out of sight.

LARK A boat; a piece of fun; looking for something to steal; on a lark.

LARREY Cunning.

LATHY Not fat. "I touched the joskin's skin, but it was as lathy as his jaws were lantern," I stole the country-man's purse, but it was as thin as his face.

LATITAT Attorney.

LAVENDER COVE A pawnbroker.

LAW "Give the cove law," give the fellow a chance to escape.

LAY A particular kind of rascality, trade, or profession; on the look out; watching for something to steal. Some-times the same as gait. "What's the cove's lay?" "Why, you see, he is on the ken's crack" — house-breaking.

LEAF Autumn. "I will be out in the leaf," I will be out in the autumn.

LEAK To impart a secret.

LEAKY Not trustworthy.

LEAP THE BOOK A false marriage.

LEAST Keep out of the way; hide; out of sight.

LEATHER A pocket-book; portmon-naie. "The bloke lost his leather," the man lost his pocket-book.

LEERY On guard; look out; wide awake.

LEFT-HANDED WIFE A concubine. It was an ancient custom among the Germans for a man, if he married his concubine, to give her his left hand, instead of the right.

LEG A gambler.

LEG-BAIL AND LAND SECURITY Runaway.

LEGGED Full-fettered; double-ironed.

LEG IT Run away; clear out.

LENTEN Nothing to eat; starving.

LETCH Unusual fastenings to a door.

LIB Sleep. "The coves lib together," the fellows sleep together.

LIBBEGE A bed.

LIBBEN A private house.

LIBKEN A lodging-house.

LICK To coax.

LIFE-PRESERVER A slung-shot.

LIFT Help. "Lift the poor cove, he is almost lenten," help the poor fellow, he is almost starved.

LIFTERS Crutches.

LIG A bedstead.

LIGHT-HOUSE A man with a very red nose.

LIGHT MANS The day.

LIL A pocket-book.

LILL A bad bill.

LILLY WHITE A chimney-sweep; a negro.

LIMB A lawyer, or lawyer's clerk.

LIMBS A long-legged fellow.

LIMBO A prison.

LINGO Talk; language.

LION Be saucy; lion the fellow; make a loud noise; substitute noise for good sense; frighten; bluff.

LISTENERS Ears.

LIVE EELS Fields. "Bill has gone to live eels, to read and write with Joe." *See Read.*

LOB A money-drawer; the till.

LOBLAY Robbing money-drawers.

LOBSNEAK A fellow that robs money-drawers.

LOCK Sometimes a receiver of stolen money; a character. "The cove stood a queer lock," the fellow had a bad character.

LOLL The favorite child; the mother's darling.

LOLLOP Lazy.

LOLLOP FEVER Lazy fever.

LONG A large price.

LONG-GONE Sentenced for life.

LOO For the good of all.

LOOBY An ignorant fellow; a fool.

LONG-TAILED-ONES Bank bills for large amount.

LOPE Run; be off. "The cove loped down the dancers, and got off with the wedge-feeders," the thief leaped down the stairs, and got away with the silver spoons.

LORD LOVEL A spade or shovel.

LOUNGE The prisoner's box in a criminal court.

LOWING-LAY Stealing cattle, oxen, or cows.

LOWRE Coin.

LOW TIDE Very little money left.

LUGGER A sailor.

LUGS Ears.

LULLABY KID An infant.

LULLIES Wet linen.

LULLIE-PRIGGERS Thieves who rob clothes-lines.

LUMBS Too many; too much.

LUMP To beat. "Lump the booby," flog the fool.

LUMP OF LEAD A bullet; sometimes the head.

LUMPING THE LIGHTER Transported.

LUMBER To walk; to walk in a careless, unconcerned manner.

LUMBER To receive stolen property from a thief for safe keeping, or disposing of it for his benefit.

LUMBERER A pawnbroker.

LUMBERER CRIB A pawnbroker's shop.

LUN The funny fellow; a clown.

LUNAN A girl.

LURCH Abandon. "Lurch the booby, he has leaked his insides out to the coppers," abandon the fool, he has told the officers all he knows.

LURRIES Valuables; watches; rings; money.

LUSH Drink.

LUSHINGTONS Drunken men.

LUSHY Drunk. "The bang-up kiddies had a spree, and got bloody lushy," the dashing boys had a party, and got very drunk.

LUSTRES Diamonds.

LYE Urine.

M

MAB A harlot.

MACE COVE A false pretense man;
a swindler; "On the mace," to live by
swindling.

MADAME A kept mistress.

MADAM RHAN A bad woman; a
strumpet.

MADE Stolen. "The copper asked me
where I made the benjamin. I told him
I didn't make it, but got it on the
square," the officer asked me where I
stole the coat, and I told him that I did
not steal it, but got it honestly.

MAD TOM A fellow who feigns to be
foolish.

MADGE Private places.

MAGG A half-cent.

MAGGING Getting money by cheating countrymen with balls, patent
safes, etc., etc.

MAGSMEN Fellows who are too cowardly to steal, but prefer to cheat confiding people by acting upon their
cupidity.

MAKE HIM SWIM FOR IT Cheat
him out of his share.

MANDERER A beggar.

MAN-TRAP A widow.

MARKING Observing; taking notice.

MARRIED Two fellows handcuffed together.

MATER Mother.

MAUDLING Crying.

MAULD Very drunk.

MAUNDING Asking alms; soliciting.

MAWKS A slattern.

MAWLEY Hand. "Tip us your mawley," tip us your hand.

MAX Gin; intoxicating liquor.

MAZZARD The face.

MEASURE To examine closely. "The copper snapped and measured me, but could not drop to my chant or mug, and so he turned me up, and I moved my beaters like a bull," the officer examined me, but could not recollect my name or face, and then let me go, and I moved my boots like a locomotive.

MEDLAR A fellow that smells bad.

MELLOW Good-natured; a little intoxicated.

MELT To spend money. "The cove melted a finniff in lush before we parted," the fellow spent five dollars for drink before we parted.

MERKIN Hair-dye.

MESTING Dissolving; melting.

MIDDLE-PIECE The stomach.

MILCH COW A man that is easily cheated out of his money.

MILKY White.

MILKY DUDS White clothes.

MILL The treadmill; a fight; a chisel.

MILL DOSE Working in prison.

MILLING COVE A pugilist. "How the milling cove served out the cull," how the boxer beat the man.

MILL LAY Breaking into houses; on the crack.

MILLER A fighter.

MILL THE GLAZE Break the window. A young thief who had turned State's evidence gave his testimony to the officer as follows: "Jack and Sneaky bustled in front of the jigger. Jack dingged Sneaky's castor into the crib; Sneaky brushed to get it; Jack pulled the jigger to, and Smasher milled the glaze, touched the swag, and mizzled like a bull, and, ye see, I played shady to pipe the bloke what was done," Jack and Sneaky pretended to scuffle in front of the shop-door. Jack pulled off Sneaky's hat and threw it into the store; Sneaky rushed in to get it; Jack, in the meantime, pulled the door to. Smasher broke the window, stole the jewelry, and was off like a locomotive. I remained near by to watch and see what steps the man would take to recover his property.

MILL TOG A shirt.

MILKEN A house-breaker.

MINNIKON Very small.

MINT Plenty of money.

MISCHIEF A man with his wife on his back.

MISS A mistress.

MISH A shirt.

MISH-TOPPER A coat or petticoat.

MIX-METAL A silver-smith.

MIZZLE Go; run; be off.

MOABITES Constables.

MOBILITY The mob; opposition to nobility.

MOBS A number of thieves working together.

MOEY A petition. A convict would say to another: "My pals have got up a bene moey to send to the head bloke, and if it comes off rye buck, I shall soon vamose from the stir; but if it should turn out a shise, then I must do my bit," my partners have got up a good petition to send to the Governor, and if it turns out well, I shall soon leave the prison; but if it should be good for nothing, I must stay my time out.

MOHAIR An upholsterer.

MOIETY Fifty.

MOKE A negro.

MOLL A woman.

MOLL BUZZER A thief that devotes himself to picking the pockets of women.

MOLLEY A miss; a young woman; an effeminate fellow; a sodomite.

MOLL-SACK Reticule.

MONDONGO Filthy; full of stench, it stinks beyond the power of endurance.

MONEKER A name.

MONEY A private place.

MOON One month; thirty days' imprisonment. "The poor cove was done for two stretches and six moons," the poor fellow was sentenced for two years and six months.

MOON-EYED HEN A squinting prostitute.

MORNING DROP The gallows. "He napped the Governor's stiff, and escaped the morning drop," he received the Governor's pardon, and escaped the gallows.

MORRIS Move off; dance off.

MORT A woman.

MOSES A man that fathers another man's child for a consideration.

MOSH Dining at an eating-house and leaving without making payment.

MOSS Money. "A rolling stone gathers no moss."

MOPSEY A short dowdy woman.

MOPUSSES Money.

MOOSE-FACE A rich, ugly-faced man; a poor but handsome young girl who marries an old, wrinkle-faced, ill-looking rich man, is said to have married a moose-face.

MOUNT To give false testimony.

MOUNTER Men who give false bail; or who, for a consideration, will swear to any thing required.

MOUNTERS Fellows who hire clothes to wear for a particular occasion; those who wear second-hand clothes.

MOUSE Be quiet; be still; talk low; whisper; step light; make no noise; softly.

MOUTH A noisy fellow; a silly fellow.

MOUTH IT Speak loud.

MOUTHING Crying. "The mort is mouthing," the girl is crying.

MOVED Bowed to. "The swell moved to the Moll as they crossed," the gentleman bowed to the girl as they passed each other.

MOW To kiss. "The bloke was mowing the molly," the man was kissing the girl.

MUCK Money.

MUCK-WORM A miser.

MUD A fool.

MUFFLERS Boxing-gloves.

MUG The face; a simple fellow.

MULL To spend money.

MUM Say nothing; nothing to say.

MUMMER The mouth.

MUMPERS Beggars.

MUND Mouth.

MUNG To solicit; to beg.

MUNS The face. "Tout the mab's muns," look at the woman's face.

MUSH An umbrella.

MUSHROOM-FAKERS Umbrella hawkers.

MUSIC The verdict of a jury when they find "not guilty."

MUSS A quarrel; a row.

MT Empty. "The bloke's leather was M T," the man's pocket-book had nothing in it — was empty.

MY UNCLE A pawnbroker.

N

NABBED Arrested.

NABCHEAT A hat.

NABGIRDER A bridle.

NABS Coxcombs.

NACKY Ingenious.

NAIDER Nothing; can't have it.

NAILED Fixed; secured; taken; arrested.

NAMASED Ran away; got out of sight; ran.

NAP To cheat.

NAPPER A cheat; a thief; the head.

NARP A shirt.

NARY Not. "I frisked the joskin's sacks, but nary red was there," I searched the countryman's pockets, but not a cent was there.

NASK A prison.

NATTY KIDS Young thieves; smart, well-dressed youngsters.

NATURAL Not fastidious; a liberal, clever fellow. "The bloke is very natural," the fellow is very liberal.

NAZY Drunken.

NAZY COVES Drunken fellows.

NAZY NOBS Drunken coxcombs or fops.

NEB The face.

NECKWEED Hemp.

NED A ten-dollar gold piece.

NEDDY A slung-shot.

NEGLIGEE A woman with nothing on but her shift.

NEMAN Stealing.

NERVE Courage; endurance; staunch.

NESCIO No; I know not; can't say.

NETTLED Diseased.

NEW LIGHT New coin; new money.

NIB The mouth.

NICK To cut. "The knuck nicked the bloke's kicks into the bottom of his poke, and the dummy fell into his mauley," the pickpocket cut through the man's pants into the bottom of his pocket, when the pocket-book dropped into his hand. This mode of stealing is only practised by the artists of the fraternity.

NICKEY The devil; "Old Nick."

NIDERING Bad; without mitigation of any kind.

NIG To clip.

NIL Nothing.

NIM To steal.

NIMENOG A very silly fellow.

NIPPERS An instrument for turning a key on the outside of the door, used by hotel-thieves.

NIPPERED Turning a key in the inside of a door, from the outside, with a peculiar pair of forceps or nippers. Hotel-thieves use nippers to enter rooms after the inmates have gone to sleep.

NIPPER-KIN   A tumbler; a drinking vessel.

NIQUE Contempt; don't care.

NISH Keep quiet; be still.

NIX Nothing.

NOB One who stands at the head; a king; a man of rank.

NOBLERS Confederates of thimble-riggers, who appear to play, to induce the flats to try their luck with the "little joker."

NOCKY BOY A simpleton.

NOD Asleep. "Gone to the land of Nod," gone to sleep.

NODDLE An empty-pated fellow; a fool; the head of an animal.

NONSENSE Melting butter in a wig.

NOOSED Married.

NOPE A blow.

NOSE A spy; one who informs. "His pal nosed, and the bene cove was pulled for crack," his partner informed against him, and the good fellow was arrested for burglary.

NOSEMY Tobacco.

NOTCH A pocket.

NOTE A singer.

NOUSE-BOX The head.

NOZZLE A chimney.

NUB The neck.

NUBBING Hanging.

NUBIBUS In the clouds. "Blow a nubibus," make a smoke.
NUG Dear. "My nug," my dear.
NULL To flog.
NUMS Sham; not real.
NYPPER A cut-purse, so called by a
person named Wotton, who in the year
1585, kept in London an academy for
the education and perfection of rogues
in the art of abstracting purses and
pocket-books. At that period persons
wore their purses at their girdles. Cutting them was a branch of the light-fin-
gered art, which is now out of use,
though the name remains. Instruction
in the practice of this art was given as
follows: A purse and a pocket were
separately suspended, attached to
which, both around and above them,
were small bells; each contained count-
ers, and he who could withdraw a
counter without causing any of the
bells to ring, was adjudged to be a
"Nypper." A nypper was a pick-purse;
a pick-pocket was called a "Foyster."

O

OAF A silly fellow.

OAFISH Simple.

OAK Strong; rich; good reputation.

OAK TOWEL An oaken cudgel.

OAR Meddle with.

OCCUPY To wear. "The cove occupies the oaf's benjamin," the fellow wears the silly man's coat.

OCHIVES Bone-handled knives.

OCHRE Money.

OFFICE Information conveyed by a look, word, or in any way by which the person receiving it is intelligibly impressed. "The cove tipped the office, and I was fly to the cop," the fellow gave me the hint, and then I knew it was a policeman.

OFFICING Signalizing; a preconcerted signal by a confederate.

OGLES The eyes.

OGLE THE COVE Look at the fellow.

OIL OF BARLEY Strong beer.

O. K. All right; "Oll kerect."

OLD Death.

OLD DOSS The Tombs.

OLD TOAST A smart old man.

OLD ONE The Devil.

OLD POGER The Devil.

OLD SHOE Good Luck.

OLIVER The moon.

OLIVER'S SKULL A chamber-pot.

OLLI COMPOLLI The chief rogue; a very smart thief.

ON A STRING To send a person to look for something that you are sure is in some other place, is putting him on a string, or humbugging, fooling him.

ON HIS MUSCLE "The fellow travels on his muscle," he presumes on his abilities to fight.

ON IT "On the cross," getting a living by other than honest means.

ON THE MUSCLE On the fight; a fighter; a pugilist.

ON THE MACE Ready to cheat; cheating for a living; a professional cheat.

ON THE SHARP Persons who are well acquainted with the mysteries of gaming, and therefore not easily cheated.

ON THE SHALLOW Half-naked.

OPTIME Class. "He's optime No. one as a screwsman," he is a first-class burglar.

ORACLE To plan a robbery or any kind of deceit.

ORGAN Pipe. "Will you lush and cock an organ with me, my bene cove?" will you drink and smoke a pipe with me, my good fellow?

96

OSTLER House thief.

OTTOMISED To be dissected. "The bene cove was scragged, ottomised, and put in a glass case for oafs to ogle," the good fellow was hung, dissected, and put in a glass case for fools to gaze at.

OTTOMY A skeleton.

OUTS Ex-officers.

OUT-AND-OUT A spree; a frolic.

OUT-AND-OUTER Distinguished; first-class.

OUTSIDER Not in the secret; not of our party.

OUTSIDE PAL The thief that watches outside when his confederates are working within.

OUTSIDE PLANT A sly place in which the receiver generally keeps his goods after purchasing.

OVEN A large mouth. "The bloke should be a baker — twig his oven," the man should be a baker — look at his big mouth.

OWLS Women who walk the streets only at night.

OWLERS Smugglers.

O YES To cry out. "The O yes of beef was rushing out of his oven like steam from a bull," the cry of stop thief was rushing out of his big mouth like steam from a locomotive.

P

PACKET A false report.

PAD A street; highway, "To go on the pad," to go on the street.

PAD THE HOOF Walk the street; to be off.

PADDING KEN A lodging-house.

PAIR OF WINGS A pair of oars.

PALAVER Talk; flattery; conference.

PAL A companion; the partner of a thief.

PALLIARDS Female mendicants who beg with a number of children, borrowing from others of the same fraternity if they have not enough of their own, giving an opiate to one to make it sleep, pinching and sticking pins into another to make it cry, and making artificial sores on the arms, hands, and face of a third, all to move the hand of the benevolent from their purses to the outstretched hand of the beggar.

PALLING IN A connection formed by a male and female thief to steal and sleep together.

PALM To fee or bribe.

PALMER A thief that adroitly slips jewelry from the top of a show-case into his pocket.

PAM A knave.

PANNAM Bread.

PANNY A house. "The cove done the panny," the fellow robbed the house; "the cops frisked my panny and nailed my screws," the officers searched my house and seized my picklocks, or false keys.

PANTER The heart. "The lead reached the poor cove's panter, and so there was nothing to be done but to give him a ground sweat," the bullet entered the poor fellow's heart, and all that we had then to do was to put him in the grave.

PANEL-CRIB A place especially and ingeniously fitted up for the robbery of gentlemen who are enticed thereto by women who make it their business to pick up strangers. Panel-cribs are sometimes called badger-cribs, shakedowns, touch-cribs, and are variously fitted for the admission of those who are in the secret, but which defy the scrutiny of the uninitiated. Sometimes the casing of the door is made to swing on well-oiled hinges which are not discoverable in the room, while the door itself appears to be hung in the usual manner, and well secured by bolts and lock. At other times the entrance is effected by means of what appears to be an ordinary wardrobe, the back of which revolves like a turn-style on pivots in the middle above and below. When the victim has undressed himself and got into bed with the woman, the thief enters, and picking the pocket-book out of the pocket, abstracts the money, and supplying its place with a small roll of paper, returns the book to its place. He then withdraws, and coming to the door raps and demands admission, calling the woman by the name of wife. The frightened victim, springing out of bed, dresses himself in a hurry, feels his pocket-book in its proper place, and escapes through another door, congratulating himself on his happy deliverance. He soon, however, finds out that he has been victimized, and not unfrequently tells the story of his loss and shame to the police; while others, minus their cash, pocket the dear-bought experience.

PANEL-THIEF One who fits up a place for the purpose of robbing men that are brought to the panel-crib by women who are trained to pick up gentlemen that are on a visit to the city on business or pleasure. They endeavor to select those who are not likely to remain and prosecute the thieves that have robbed and duped them of their money.

PANZY A burglar.

PAPER-SKULL A thin-skulled fellow.

PAP LAP An infant. "He is but a pap lap," he is but a baby.

PARCHMENT A ticket of leave. "The cove has his parchment," the man has his ticket of leave.

PARCHMENT COVES Ticket-of-leave men.

PARELL To make clear.

PARNEY A ring.

PARK RAILING The teeth.

PARSON A guide-post.

PARTIAL Putting one's hand into another man's pocket; stealing.

PASH Price; cost.

PATE The head.

PATTER To talk. "How the Moll lushes her jockey and patters," how the girl drinks her gin and talks.

PATTERED Tried in a court of justice. "The wire was pattered for drawing a skin from a bloke's poke, who buffed him home, and of course his godfathers named him, and the beak slung him for five stretchers and a moon," the pickpocket was tried for stealing a purse from the man's pocket, who caught him in the act, and of course the jury convicted him, and the judge sentenced him for five year and a month.

PATRICO One who in olden time used to marry persons by placing the

man on the right hand side and the
woman on the left side of a dead animal. Causing them to join hands, he
commanded them to live together till
death did them part, and so, shaking
hands, the wedding was ended.

PAUM To conceal in the hand. "To
paum penny-weights," to steal rings or
any kind of jewelry by working it with
the fingers under the palm of the hand,
and then up the sleeve or into a pocket.
These fellows are called paum-coves.

PAW The hand or foot. "The fore-
paw hand;" "the hind paw foot."

PEACH To inform; "to turn stag;" to
blow the gab; to squeal or squeak.

PEAK Lace goods.

PEAL A ball.

PEAR To draw supplies from both
sides; to give the officers information,
and then tell the thieves to get out of
the way.

PEAR-MAKING The act of drawing
supplies from both sides. *See Pear.*

PECCAVI I have sinned; I am
wrong; a confession of wrong.

PECK Food.

PECK AND BOOZE Food and drink.

PECKISH Hungry.

PECULIAR A mistress.

PED A basket.

PEDDLER'S PONY A walking-stick.

PEEL Strip; undress.

PEEPER A spy-glass; an opera-glass; a looking-glass. "Track up the dancers and pike with the peeper," jump up stairs and run off with the looking-glass.

PEEPERS Eyes.

PEEPING TOM A curious, prying fellow, who minds other people's business more than his own.

PEEPY Drowsy.

PEER To look cautiously about; to be circumspect; careful.

PEERY Suspicious. "The bloke's peery," the man suspects something. "There's a peery, 'tis snitch," we are observed, nothing can be done.

PEGTANTRUM Dead.

PELT A passion; rage. "What a pelt the cull is in," what a passion the fellow is in.

PENNYWEIGHT Jewelry; gold and silver trinkets.

PEPPERY Warm; passionate.

PERSUADERS Spurs. "The kiddy clapped his persuaders to his prad, but it was no go, the trap boned him," the highwayman spurred his horse hard, but the officer seized him.

PETER A portmanteau; a travelling-bag; a trunk; an iron chest; a cash-box.

PETER-BITER A man who steals baggage at hotels, railroad depots, and from the back of coaches.

PHARO Strong malt liquor.

PHARSE The eighth part.

PHILISTINES Police officers; officers of justice.

PHIZ The face. "A rum phiz," an odd face.

PHYSOG The face.

PICAROON A sharper; a rogue.

PICKLE A smart fellow.

PICKLING Stealing; petit larceny.

PICKLING-TUBS Shoes and boots.

PICTURE-FRAME The gallows.

PIECE A prostitute.

PIG A police officer. "Floor the pig and bolt," knock down the officer and run away.

PIGEON A thief that joins in with other thieves to commit a crime, and then informs the officer, who he pigeons for; and for this service the officer is supposed to be *occasionally* both deaf and blind.

PIG'S EYES Small eyes.

PIG'S FOOT A jimmy cloven at one end like a pig's foot.

PIG TOGETHER Sleep together, two or more in a bed.

PIG WIDGEON A simple fellow.

PIKE To run away; to pike off.

PILCHER A stealer; generally applied to fellows who steal pocket-handkerchiefs.

PILGARLIC I; myself. "There was no one with him but Pilgarlic," he was alone.

PIMP A boarding-house runner; an attaché of a bawdy-house.

PIMPLE The head.

PIN To drink one's allotted share.

PINNED Arrested.

PINS Legs.

PIN-BASKET The youngest child; the baby.

PINCH To steal.

PINCHED Arrested.

PINCHERS Sometimes called "Exchangers;" fellows who go into stores or exchange offices with a twenty-dollar gold coin and ask to have it changed for bank bills, and after receiving the bills, suddenly pretend to have changed their minds, and, handing the bills back again, make very profuse apologies for the trouble they have given, etc., etc. The man during the short time that he had the money in his possession, contrived to change bad bills for some of the good ones.

PINK To stab.

PINKED Stabbed.

PINKED BETWEEN THE LACINGS Convicted by reason of perjury. A man encased in a steel or iron is only vulnerable at those parts where his corselet is laced; and hence when an honest man is convicted of a false charge by a treacherous advantage of some weak point, he is said to be "pinked between the lacings."

PIN-MONEY Money received by a married woman for prostituting her person.

PINNIPE A crab.

PINNIPED Sideways; crab-fashion.

PIPER A short-winded person; a broken-winded horse.

PIPING Following; trailing; dogging; looking after; watching.

PIT A pocket.

PLAIUL Go home.

PLANT To bury; to conceal. Stolen goods are said to be planted when they are concealed. "Plant your wids and stow them," be careful what you say.

PLANTER One who hides stolen property.

PLANTING Hiding; concealing.

PLASTIC A model artist.

PLATE Money.

PLATE OF MEAT A street or highway.

PLAYED OUT Exhausted; expended.

PLAYTHINGS Burglar's tools.

PLUCK To pull.

PLUCK THE RIBBON Pull the bell.

PLUMB Honest; upright; good.

PLUMBY It is all right, or as it should be; we have plenty; they have enough.

PLUMP Rich; plenty of money. "A plump skin," a full purse.

PLYER A crutch.

POGY Drunk.

POINT To pay.

POKE A pocket; a purse.

POLISHER One who is in prison. "The cove polishes the people's iron with his eyebrows," the fellow looks out of the grated windows of his prison.

POLL The head.

POLL HIM Get hold of the property, and then refuse to pay for it.

POLT A blow. "Lend the pam a polt in the muns," give the fool a blow in the face.

POMP The game. "Save the pomp," save the game.

PONCE A man who is kept by a woman.

PONCESS A woman that keeps a man by prostitution.

POND The ocean.

PONEY Money. "Post the poney," put down the money.

PONGELO Drink; liquor.

POP To pawn; to shoot.

POPS Pistols. "I popped the bloke," I shot the fellow.

POPSHOP Pawnbroker's shop.

PORK To inform the coroner of the whereabouts of a corpse.

PORKER A saddle. Saddles are mostly made of hog's skins.

PORT ST. MARTIN A valise; a portmanteau.

POSH Money; smallest piece of money.

POST Pay; put up.

POST THE COLE Pay the money.

POT-HUNTER A poor person who steals food only to prevent himself from starving.

POULTERER A fellow who opens letters, abstracts the money and then drops them back into the post-office box. "The kiddy was pulled for the poultry rig," the boy was arrested for opening letters and robbing them.

POUCH A pocket.

PRAD A horse.

PRAD-BORROWERS Horse-thieves.

PRAD-LAY Stealing horses.

PRANCER A horse.

PRATE ROAST A talkative fellow.

PRATER A hen.

PRATING CHEAT The tongue.

PRATT Back parts.

PREMONITORY The penitentiary.

PRIG A thief.

PRIGGER-NAPPER A police officer.

PRIGGERS Thieves in general.

PRIGSTAR A rival in a love affair.

PRIM A handsome woman.

PRIME TWIG First-rate condition.

PROD A cart or wagon; a coach.

PROG Food.

PROP A breast-pin.

PROPS Dice.

PROSPECTING Looking for something to steal.

PUFFERS Peter Funks.

PULL To arrest. To "pull a purse," is to steal a purse.

PUNCH A blow struck with the fist. "A punch in the day-light, the victualling-office, or the haltering place," a blow in the eye, the stomach, or under the ear.

PUNK A bad woman.

PUPPY Blind.

PUSH A crowd.

PUT An ignorant clown.

PUT AWAY Locked up; imprisoned.

PUT A FELLOW UP TO HIS ARM-PITS Cheated by his companions of his share of the plunder.

PUT TO BED WITH A SHOVEL Buried in the earth.

PUT UP Information given to thieves by persons in the employ of parties to be robbed, such as servants, clerks, porters, etc., whereby the thief is facilitated in his operations.

PUT UP JOB A job is said to be put up if the porter of a store should allow a "fitter" to take an impression of the keys of the door or the safe; or when a clerk sent to the bank to make a deposit, or to draw an amount of money, allows himself to be thrown down and robbed, in order to have his pocket picked.

PUZZLE-COVE A lawyer.

Q

QUACKING-CHEAT A duck.

QUAG Unsafe; not reliable; not to be trusted.

QUAIL An old maid.

QUAIL-PIPE A woman's tongue.

QUAKING-CHEAT A calf or a sheep.

QUANDARY What shall I do.

QUARREL-PICKER A glazier.

QUARROON A body.

QUARTERED To receive a part of the profits.

QUASH To kill; the end of; no more.

QUEAN A slut; a worthless woman.

QUEEN DICK Never. "It happened in the reign of Queen Dick," it never occurred; has never been.

QUEEN STREET "The joskin lives in Queen Street," the fool is governed entirely by his wife.

QUEER Counterfeit bank bills; base; roguish; worthless.

QUEER To puzzle. "The cove queered the full bottom," the fellow puzzled the judge. "The bloke queered his ogles among the bruisers," he had his eyes blacked by the pugilists.

QUEER BIRDS Reformed convicts who return to their old profession.

QUEER BLUFFER The keeper of a rum-shop that is the resort of the worst kind of rogues, and who assists them in various ways.

QUEER BURY An empty purse.

QUEER COLE FENCER A passer of bad money.

QUEER COLE MAKER One who makes bad money.

QUEER PRANCER A bad horse.

QUEER ROOSTER A fellow that lodges among thieves to hear what they have to say, and then imparts his information to officers for a consideration.

QUEMAR Burn the fellow.

QUES Points.

QUIDS Cash; five dollars. "The swell tipped the mace cove fifty quids for the prad," the gentleman gave fifty dollars for the horse.

QUINSEY Choke. "Quinsey the bloke while I frisk his sacks," choke the fellow while I pick his pockets.

QUOD Prison.

QUOTA Share. "Tip me my quota," give me my share.

R

RABBIT A rowdy. "Dead rabbit," a very athletic rowdy fellow.

RABBIT-SUCKERS Young spend-thrifts; fast young men.

RACKLAW A married woman.

RAG A dollar. "Not a rag," not a dollar.

RAGGED Abused; slandered.

RAGS Paper money. "Poor cove, rags are few with him," poor fellow, money is not plenty with him.

RAG-WATER Intoxicating liquor of all kinds. If frequently taken to excess, will reduce any person to rags.

RAILS Curtain lectures.

RAINBOW A footman; so called from the fact that he wears livery, or garments of different colors.

RAINY DAY A day of sickness; a day of want; bad times and rainy days.

RAKE To apportion; share.

RALPH A fool.

RAMMER The arm. "The cooper seized my rammer, and run me like a prad to the wit," the officer laid hold of my arm, and ran me like a horse to prison.

RAMP To snatch; to tear any thing forcibly from the person. Pickpockets are said to be ramping a man when a number of them rush on him as if in a great hurry to pass, but manage to run against him, and in the flurry pick his pocket.

RANCAT COVE A man covered with fur.

RANDY Unruly; rampant.

RANGLING Intriguing with a number of women.

RAP To take a false oath; to curse.

RAPPER A perjurer.

RASCAGLION A eunuch.

RAT A trick; a cheat. "To smell a rat," to suspect.

RATTLE A hackney coach.

RATTLING COVE A coachman.

READ AND WRITE Flight. "He took to read and write with Joe in Daisyville."

READER A pocket-book.

READER MERCHANTS Pickpockets who operate in and about the banks.

READY Cash.

RECKON Cheat.

RECRUITING Thieves hunting for plunder.

RED Gold; a cent.

RED SUPER A gold watch.

RED FUSTIAN Porter or red wine.

REDGE Gold.

RED RAG The tongue. "Shut your potato-trap and give the red rag a holiday," shut your mouth and let your tongue rest.

RED LANE The throat.

REEFING Drawing. "Reefing up into work," drawing up the pocket until the purse or portmonnaie is within reach of the fingers.

REGULARS Share or portion. "The coves cracked the swell's crib, fenced the swag, and then each bloke napped his regulars," the fellows broke open a gentleman's house, sold the goods to a receiver, and each man received his portion.

REP A man of good reputation.

REPS A woman of good reputation.

REVERSED A man made to stand on his head by rowdies, in order that his money may fall out of his pockets. It is then picked up as money found.

RIB A cross, ill-natured wife.

RIBBON Liquor.

RIB-ROAST The act of scolding a husband unmercifully by his wife.

RICHARDSNARY A dictionary.

RED RIBBON Brandy.

RIG Joke; fun.

RIGGING Clothing.

RIGHT All right; just as it was wished to be.

RIGHTS "To rights," clear. "Oh!
then, you are *to rights* this time," there
is a clear case against you.
RIGHT SORT One of your kind; a
good fellow.
RHINO Money.
RHINO FAT Being rich.
RING To ring in is to join in with an-
other and appear to think as he thinks;
to intrude; to force one's self into com-
pany where he is not wanted.
RIP A poor devil.
RIPPERS Spurs.
ROAST To arrest.
ROBIN'S MEN From Robin Hood.
Expert thieves; grand larceny men;
bank-robbers, etc.
ROCKED IN A STONE CRADLE
Born in a prison.
RODGER A portmanteau.
ROGUE "Rogue and pulley," a man
and woman going out to rob gentlemen.
ROLL OF SNOW A roll of linen.
ROME COVE A king; the president.
ROME MORT A queen.
ROME VILLE New-York.
ROMONERS Fortune-tellers.
ROMONEY A gipsy.
ROOFER A hat.
ROOK A cheat.
ROOST-LAY Stealing poultry.
ROPED Led astray; taken in and done
for.

ROPER-IN A man who visits hotels and other places for the purpose of ingratiating himself with persons who are supposed to have plenty of cash and little prudence, and inducing them to visit gaming-houses.

ROSE A secret.

ROTAN Any wheeled carriage.

ROUGHS Men that are ready to fight in any way or shape.

ROUGH MUSIC Noise made by beating old tins.

ROUND Good.

ROUND ABOUT An instrument used by burglars to cut a large hole into an iron chest or door.

ROUNDING Informing; giving information.

ROUND ROBIN A burglar's instrument.

ROVERS Thoughts.

RUB Run. "Don't rub us to wit," don't run us to prison.

RUB US TO WIT Send us to prison.

RUFFELS Hand-cuffs.

RUFFIAN The devil. "May the ruffian nab the cuffin queer, and let the copper twine with his kinchins around his colquarren," may the devil take the justice, and let the policeman be hanged with all his children about his neck. "The ruffian cly you," the devil take you.

RUG Sleep.

RUGG It is all right.

RUMBEAK A magistrate that can be bribed.

RUMBLE THE FLATS Playing cards.

RUMBOB A money-drawer.

RUMBING A full purse.

RUM BITE A smart cheat; a clean trick.

RUM BLOWEN A handsome girl.

RUM BLUFFER A jolly landlord.

RUMBO A prison.

RUMBOB A young apprentice.

RUMBOSE Wine or any kind of good drink.

RUMBUGHER A valuable dog.

RUM CHUB A fellow.

RUN Fine; good; valuable.

RUN IN Arrested.

RUNNING HIM THROUGH A term used by gamblers when they play with a sucker, and don't give him a chance to win a single bet.

RUSHERS House-breakers who break into country houses.

RUSTY Ill-natured. His tongue goes like a door on rusty hinges.

RYBUCK All right; straight; it will do; I am satisfied.

RYDER A cloak.

S

SACHEVEREL An iron door.

SACK A pocket.

SAINT GILES BUZZMAN A hand-kerchief thief.

SAINT TERRA A churchyard.

SAM A stupid fellow.

SANGUINARY Bloody.

SANS Without; nothing.

SAWNEY Bacon; fat pork.

SCAMP-FOOT A foot-pad.

SCANDAL PROOF One who has eaten shame and drank after it; or would blush at being ashamed.

SCANDAL SOUP Tea.

SCARCE To slip away; to make one's self scarce.

SCAVIOR Sharp; cunning; knowl-edge.

SCENT Bad management. "The cove was nabbed on the scent," the fellow was arrested by reason of his own bad management.

SCHEME A party of pleasure.

SCHOFEL Bad money.

SCHOFEL-PITCHERS Passers of bad money.

SCHOOL A gang of thieves. "A school of knucks," a gang of pickpockets.

SCHOOL OIL A whipping.

SCHOOLING Jostling; pitching.

SCOUT A watchman.

SCRAGG The neck.

SCRAGGED Hanged.

SCRAN Food.

SCRANNING Begging.

SCRAPE Trouble.

SCRAPP A plan to rob a house or commit any kind of roguery.

SCRAPPER A pugilist.

SCRATCH To write; to forge.

SCRATCHER A forger; a copyist.

SCREAVES Paper money.

SCREEN A bank-bill.

SCRUB-BADO A mean, insignificant puppy; the lowest of the low; the itch.

SCREW A key.

SCREWING Opening a lock with keys.

SCREWSMAN A burglar who works with keys, picks, dubs, bettys, etc., etc.

SCREWING UP Choking; garroting. "Screw up the bloke, and that will stop his blasted red rag from chanting beef," choke the man, and that will prevent him from crying "stop thief."

SCRUB A mean fellow.

SCRIP Writing-paper. "The bloke freely scratched the scrip, and tipped me forty cases,'' the man readily signed the paper, and gave me forty dollars.

SCOLD'S CURE A coffin. "The blowen has napped the scold's cure," the jade is in her coffin.

SCOT A young bull.

SCOUR To run away.

SCROBE A private chastisement.

SCROOF To live with a friend, and at his expense.

SCROOFING Living at a friend's expense. Thieves are in the habit of scroofing with an old pal when they first come out of prison, until they can steal something for themselves.

SCRATCH Time agreed upon; to meet at the appointed time; to face another.

SCUTTLE To cut a pocket.

SEA-CRAB A sailor.

SEAVEY Sense; knowledge.

SECRET Cheated. "The bloke was let into the secret," the man was cheated.

SEES The eyes.

SEND To drive or break. "Take the jimmy and send it into the jigger," take the crow and force it into the door.

SERENE All right. It is all serene.

SERVED Found guilty; convicted.

SERVE HIM OUT Give him a good thrashing.

SET Prepared beforehand; "a set thing;" a trap; a determined thing.

SETTLED Knocked down; murdered.

SETTLING Killing. "Settling a bloke," killing a man.

SETTER A shadow; an officer in disguise, who points out the thief for others to arrest.

SHADOW A first-class police officer; one who possesses naturally the power of retaining with unerring certainty the peculiar features and characteristics of persons, added to the indomitable perseverance of the slot-hound to follow his quarry.

SHADY Quiet; out of sight; not easily found.

SHADY GLIM A dark lantern.

SHAKE A prostitute; one who gambles with dice; to shake; to draw any thing from the pocket. "The knuck shook the swell of his fogle," the pickpocket stole the gentleman's handkerchief.

SHAKEDOWN A panel-thief or badger's crib.

SHAKESTER A lady.

SHALERS Girls.

SHALLY A negative; a person that is never positive.

SHAM LEGGERS Men who pretend to sell smuggled goods.

SHAP A hat.

SHAPES Naked.

SHARK A custom-house officer.

SHARP A man that is well posted; one who "knows a thing or two;" a gambler.

SHARPER One who obtains goods or money by any kind of false pretense or representation.

SHARPER'S TOOLS A fool and false dice or cards.

SHAVER A cheat.

SHEENEY A Jew thief.

SHELF A pawn-shop.

SHEEN Bad money.

SHELION A shilling.

SHERIFF'S BALL An execution.

SHERO The head.

SHERRID Run away.

SHICKSTER A woman.

SHIFTING Cheating or stealing.

SHIGUS A judge.

SHILLEY No stability.

SHIN-BREAKING Borrowing money.

SHINES Gold coin.

SHINERAGS Nothing.

SHOE-LEATHER A phrase to denote some one is approaching.

SHOON A fool; a country lout.

SHOOTING-STARS Thieves who do not remain long in one place.

SHOP A prison.

SHOPPED Imprisoned.

SHOVE Pass money. "Shove the blunt," spend the money. "Shove queer," pass counterfeit money.

SHOVING Passing bad money.

SHRED A tailor.

SHYCOCK A man who is fearful of being arrested; shy of the officers.

SICER Sixpence.

SICK Imprisoned.

SIDE-POCKET A drinking-saloon in an out-of-the-way-place; a resort for thieves.

SIFTING Examining; emptying purses or pocket-books for the purpose of examining their contents, is called sifting.

SILENCE To kill; to knock down.

SIMKIN A fool.

SIMON A simpleton.

SING To cry aloud. "The cove sings beef," the fellow calls thief.

SING SMALL Have little to say for yourself.

SINK To cheat; to hide from a partner.

SINKERS Thieves who do not divide fair with their companions.

SINKING Cheating a partner; not dividing fair.

SKEP A pocket full of money; a place for keeping money; a savings bank.

SKEW A cup.

SKEWER A sword or dagger.

SKILLEY Prison fare.

SKIN A purse. "The bloke's skin was full of honey," the man's purse was full of money.

SKINK A waiter.

SKINNERS Small lawyers who hang about police offices and figuratively skin their clients.

SKIP-KENNEL A footman.

SKIPPER A barn.

SKIT Humbug; a joke.

SKULL The head of the house; the President of the United States; the Governor; the head man.

SKY-BLUE Gin.

SKYCER A mean, sponging fellow.

SLANG or SLAG A watch-chain. "The knucks twisted the swell's thimble, slang, and onions, and also touched his leather, but it was very lathy. It only raked a case and a half; the thimble was a foist, but the slang and onions were bene. The altemel of the swag raked only fifteen cases," the pickpockets stole a gentleman's watch, chain, and seals, and also his pocketbook; but there was only a dollar and a half a piece for them in it. The watch was a cheat, but the chain and seals were good. The whole plunder divided gave the thieves fifteen dollars each.

SLANGED Chained by the leg.

SLAP-BANG An eating-house; a restaurant.

SLAMKIN A slovenly female.

SLANEY A theatre.

SLASH Outside coat pocket.

SLAT A half-dollar.

SLATE A sheet.

SLAWEY A female servant.

SLICK-A-DYE A pocket-book.

SLIM Punch.

SLINGTAIL Poultry.

SLIPPERY Soap.

SLOP Tea.

SLOPS Ready-made clothing.

SLOUGH To bow the head.

SLUBBER A heavy, stupid fellow.

SLUBBER DE GULLION A mean fellow.

SLUICED To drink. "The bene cove sluiced their gobs with slim till they all snoozed in the strammel like sounders," the good fellow gave them punch till they slept in the straw like hogs.

SLUICE YOUR GOB Take a good long drink.

SLUM A package of bank bills; a low drinking-place.

SLUMING Passing spurious bills.

SLUMMING Stealing packages of bank-bills.

SLY-BOOTS A fellow that pretends to be a fool.

SMACK To share. "Smack the swag," share the spoil.

SMACK To swear on the Bible. "The queer cuffin bid me smack the calf-skin, but I only bussed my thumb," the justice told me to kiss the book, but I only kissed my thumb.

SMACKING COVE A coachman.

SMALL SNOW Children's linen.

SMART Spruce.

SMASH To change.

SMASHER Money-changer.

SMASH-FEEDER A silver spoon.

SMEAR A plasterer; a mason.

SMEAR GILT A bribe.

SMELLER A nose.

SMELLING CHEAT A bouquet.

SMELT S Half-eagles; five dollars.

SMICKET A woman's shift or skirt.

SMILE To drink.

SMILER A bumper.

SMIRK A superficial fellow.

SMITER The arm.

SMOKE Humbug; any thing said to conceal the true sentiment of the talker; to cover the intent.

SMOKE To observe; to suspect; to understand.

SMOKY Suspicious; curious; inquisitive.

SMOUCH To steal.

SMUG A blacksmith.

SMUSH To seize suddenly; to snatch.

SMUT Indecent.

SNABLE To plunder; sometimes to kill.

SNAFFLERS Highwaymen.

SNAGS Large teeth.

SNAGLING Stealing poultry by putting a worm on a fish-hook, thereby catching the fowl, then twisting their necks and putting them in a bag.

SNAKE A fellow that glides into a store or warehouse, and conceals himself for the purpose of letting in his companions.

SNAKED Arrested.

SNAM To snatch.

SNAPPED Arrested.

SNAPPER A gun.

SNAPPERS Pistols.

SNAPT Arrested; caught.

SNEAK-THIEF A fellow who sneaks into areas, basement-doors or windows, or through front-doors by means of latch-keys and entering the various apartments, steals any thing he can carry off.

SNEAKING Conveying away stolen goods.

SNEAKSMAN *See Sneak-thief.*

SNEEZER A snuff-box.

SNID Six.

SNIDE STUFF Bad money.

SNITCH An informer; the nose; a spy.

SNITE Slap; wipe. "Snite his snitch," wipe his nose.

SNIVEL To cry.

SNOOZING-KEN A bawdy-house.

SNOT A gentleman.

SNOUT A hogshead.

SNOW Linen.

SNUDGE A thief who conceals himself under the bed.

SNUFF Offended. "To take snuff," to be offended.

SNUG Quiet; all right.

SOAP Money.

SOD A worn-out debauchee, whom excess of indulgence has rendered unnatural.

SOFT Bank bills; paper money.

SOLDIER A smoked herring.

SOLFA A clerk.

SOP A bribe.

SOT-WEED Tobacco.

SOUNDERS Hogs.

SPADO A sword.

SPANISH Silver coin.

SPARK A diamond.

SPEAK To steal; to take away. "Bob spoke with the toney on the chestnut prancer," Bob robbed the fool on the chestnut horse. "To speak with," to steal from.

SPEAKER Plunderer.

SPEALERS Gamblers.

SPEILER A gambler.

SPEILING Gambling.

SPICE To steal.

SPICER A foot-pad.

SPICER HIGH A highway-robber.

SPIT A sword or dagger.

SPLIT Parted; separated.

SPLIT CAUSE A lawyer.

SPLIT ON HIM Informs against; denounces him.

SPLIT OUT No longer friends; quarrelled; dissolved partnership.

SPOONEY Foolish.

SPORT A gamester; a man fond of racing and gaming of all kinds.

SPOT To make a note of something you wish to remember; to look at a person with the intention of remembering him; to point one out to another as a suspected person, or one to be remembered.

SPOUT A pawnbroker's shop.

SPRAT Sixpence.

SPREAD Butter. "The cove pinched a keeler of spread, and was pulled foul. The beaks sent him to the premonitory for three moons," the fellow stole a tub of butter, and was arrested with it in his possession. The judges sent him to the penitentiary for three months.

SPRINGING THE PLANT To discover the place where stolen property is concealed; to remove stolen property from its place of concealment. "When I was in the old doss I told my skinner to see Jack and tell him to spring the plant, fence it, and send me my regulars, as I wanted to melt it," when I was in the Tombs I told my lawyer to see Jack, and tell him to remove the plunder from the place in which we hid it, to sell it, and send me my share of the proceeds, as I wanted to spend it.

SPUD Base coin; bad money.

SPUNG A miser.

SPUNK Matches.

SPUNK-FAKERS Match-sellers.

SQUARE Honest; upright; good.

SQUEAK or SQUEAL To inform. A thief is said to "squeak" or "squeal" when, after his arrest, he gives information against his accomplices, or where stolen property may be found.

SQUEAKER A child.

SQUAIL A drink.

SQUEEZE Silk or satin.

SQUEEZE CLOUT A silk handkerchief.

SQUELCH A fall.

STAG One who has turned State's evidence.

STAG To see. "Stag the cop," see the policeman.

STAGGED Discovered; informed on.

STAIT City of New-York.

STAKE Plunder, large or small in value, as the case may be.

STALL One whose business it is to conceal as far as possible the manipulation of his confederate who is trying to pick a person's pocket. The stall places himself either in front, back, or sideways, or by any stratagem attracts the attention of the intended victim. Any thing said or done by which the attention is directed from the true state of the case is called a *stall*.

STALLING-KEN A house for the reception of stolen goods.

STAMFISH To talk in a way not generally understood.

STANDING Purchasing stolen property.

STANDING IN Bidding for; making an offer; taking part with. "The bloke stands in with the cross-coves, and naps his regulars," the man takes part with the thieves, and receives his share of the plunder.

STAMP A particular way of throwing dice out of the box.

STAMPERS Feet; shoes; sometimes the stairs.

STARCH Pride.

STARDER A receiver.

STAR-GAZERS Prostitutes; street-walkers.

STARK NAKED Stripped of everything; "skinned by a Tombs lawyer."

STAR THE GLAZE Break the showcase; break the glass.

START The Tombs. "The cove has gone to the old start," the fellow has gone to the Tombs.

STAUNCH Can not be made to tell; reliable; can be trusted with a secret. "I say, Smasher, Won't the cove squeak if he's pinched and promised by the beak to be turned up?" "No, not for all the blasted beaks this side of Sturbin. I tell you he is a staunch cove, and there need be no fear," I say, Smasher, won't the fellow betray us if he is arrested and promised by the judge to be set at liberty again? No, not for all the blasted judges this side of State prison. I tell you he is a reliable fellow, and there is no fear.

STAY-TAPE A dry-goods clerk.

STEAMER A tobacco pipe.

STEEL House of Refuge.

STEPPER The treadmill.

STEPPING-KEN A dance-house.

STICK A breastpin.

STICK-FLAMS Gloves.

STICKS Pistols; household furniture.

STIFF A letter; a written or printed paper; a newspaper.

STIFF 'UN A corpse.

STIFLE Kill.

STIFLE THE SQUEAKER Kill the child.

STINK To publish an account of a robbery.

STIR A crowd; a fire.

STOGGER A pickpocket.

STONE PITCHER Sing Sing.

STOP A detective officer.

STOP LAY Two or more well-dressed pickpockets go into a fashionable quiet street and promenade singly until they select a person that will answer their purpose; one of them stops the person and inquires the direction to a place somewhat distant. On being informed of the route he should take, he pretends not to exactly understand his inform-ant, who, getting a little more inter-ested in his desire to be explicit, draws closer to the inquirer. At about this point, one or both of the others walk up and in an instant the amiable individ-ual is minus some part of his movable property. The above practice is what is termed the "stop lay."

STOW YOUR WID Be silent.

STRAMMEL Straw; hay.

STRANGER A guinea.

STRAW-MAN False bail.

STRETCH One year.

STRETCHERS Horse-racers.

STRIKE To get money from candi-dates before an election, under the pre-tense of getting votes for them; to borrow without intending to pay back.

STRING To humbug. "String the bloke and pinch his honey," humbug the man and get his money.

STRUMMER-FEKER A hair-dresser.

STUBBLE Stop it.

STUBBLE YOUR RED RAG Hold your tongue.

STUFF Money.

STUKE A handkerchief.

STURBIN State prison.

STUMPS Legs.

STUNNER Extra; superior; very good.

STUN HIM OUT OF HIS REGU-LARS Cheat him out of his rights; deprive him of his share of the plunder.

SUBSIDE Get out of the way; run away.

SUCK Any kind of liquor.

SUCKER A term applied by gamblers to a person that can be cheated at any game of cards.

SUCKED Cheated.

SUDSDAY Washday.

SUET Liquor.

SUGAR Money.

SUITE Watch, seals, etc.

SUPER or SOUPER A watch.

SUPOUCH A landlady.

SURE THING A term used to denote that the person is certain to be a winner.

SUSPERCOL To hang.

SWABLER A dirty fellow.

SWADDLER A fellow who pretends to be anxious for the salvation of every body, and harangues crowds of gaping knaves and fools in the parks, or any other public place. The pickpockets generally pay him well for his efforts. Sometimes fellows who pick a quarrel with a man, beat him, and at the same time rob him, are called swaddlers.

SWAG Plunder.

SWAG-COVE A receiver of stolen goods.

SWAG-RUM Full of wealth.

SWEATING Reducing the weight of gold coin by putting it in a bag and shaking it violently for some time, and then collecting the dust which is thus worn off.

SWELL A gentleman. "Swell mob," the well-dressed thieves with good address, who appear like honest gentlemen.

SWIG Liquor of any kind.

SWIG-COVES Fellows who traverse the country under the pretense of begging old clothes.

SWING To hang.

SWITCHED Married.

SYEBUCK Sixpence.

SYNTAX A schoolmaster.

T

TABBY An old maid; or a talkative old woman.

TACE A candle; silence; hold your tongue.

TACKLE A mistress; sometimes clothing.

TAIL-DIVER A thief who steals pocket-handkerchiefs from coat-tail pockets.

TALE The number; quantity; share. "Give him tale," give him his share.

TALLEYMEN Men who loan clothing to prostitutes.

TANGLE-FOOT Bad liquor.

TANGLE-FOOTED Drunk.

TANNER Sixpence. "The kiddy tipped the rattling cove a tanner for lush," the lad gave the coachman sixpence to get a drink.

TAP To arrest.

TAPE Liquor.

TAPPERS Officers.

TARRELS Skeleton-keys.

TATTLER A watch or clock. "To flash a tattler," to sport a watch.

TATS False dice; rags.

TATTY-TOG A sweat-cloth.

TEASE A slave; to work.

TEEHOKOIS Dogs or dog.

TEIZE To flog. "To nap the teize," to receive a flogging.

TESTON A coin with a head on it.

THEATRE Police court.

THIMBLE A watch.

THORNS Anxious; fearful.

THRESWINS Three cents or pence.

THROUGH HIM Search him.

THROW To cheat; to rob; to steal.

THROWING OFF A term used by gamblers when a capper is the partner of a sucker. The capper can lose when he pleases, thereby throwing the sucker off, as it is termed.

THRUMS Three-cent pieces.

TIBBS A goose.

TIBBY A cat.

TICK Trust.

TICKRUM A license.

TIED UP GONNOFFING Stopped stealing; living honestly.

TIFFING A good natured war of words.

TILE A hat.

TIMBER Matches.

TIME ON THAT Wait awhile, sir; not so fast.

TIP Information; give; hand to me; lend. "Tip me your daddle, my bene cove," give me your hand, my good fellow.

TIPPET The halter.

TIT A horse.

TITTER A sword.

TIZZY Sixpence.

TOBBY COVES Fellows that in the night walk the streets near a river. They stun their victim by striking him with a bludgeon; they then rob him and tumble him into the river. If the body is found, it is difficult to say that the man was not accidentally drowned.

TOBED Struck on the head and made senseless.

TO BLOWER One who imparts secrets; to inform.

TO BLOW THE GAB To confess.

TO BREAK A LEG To seduce a girl.

TOBY The highway.

TOBY-LAY Robbing on the highway.

TODGE To smash. "Todge the bloke and pad," smoke the man and run.

TOGE A coat.

TOGS Clothes. "The swell is rum-togged," the gentleman is well dressed.

TO HAVE A GAME DEAD The gambler has a sure thing, and must beat his opponent.

TOLOBON The tongue.

TOLOBON RIG Fortune-tellers.

TOMBSTONES Teeth.

TOM-CONEY A foolish fellow.

TOMMEY Bread.

TONEY A simpleton.

TOOLS Burglars' instruments.

TOOTH-MUSIC Chewing food with a good appetite.

TOP To cheat; to trick.

TOPPED Hanged. "The cove was topped for settling a bloke," the fellow was hanged for killing a man.

TOP-DIVER A roué.

TOPPING-COVE The head man of a party; sometimes the hangman.

TOPPER A blow on the head.

TOP-ROPES Extravagant or riotous living.

TOP-TOG An overcoat.

TOTH Rum.

TO TURN STAG To turn informer.

TO BE PUT IN A HOLE To be cheated by a comrade out of a just share of the plunder.

TO BOUNCE To brag or hector; to tell improbable stories.

TO BOUNCE HIM To get one's property and refuse to pay for it.

TO RIGHTS The evidence is conclusive enough to convict. "Try all they knew, the coppers could not pinch him to rights — he was too fly for them," the officers were not able to find evidence enough against him. He was too cunning for them.

TOUCH To steal.

TONGUE-PAD A scold.

TOUT Look; take notice; remember that.

TOUTED Followed or pursued.

TOUTING-KEN The bar of a drink-ing-place.

TOWER Rage; very angry.

TOWN-TODDLERS Silly fellows eas-ily taken in by the sharpers.

TO YARD KICK Coat and pants.

TRACK To go.

TRADESMEN Thieves.

TRANSLATORS Second-hand boots or shoes.

TRAP Shrewd; smart.

TRAPES Sluttish women.

TRAPS Officers.

TRAY Three.

TRIB A prison.

TRICKS Anything stolen from a per-son at one time by pickpockets.

TRICUM LEGIS A quirk or quibble.

TRINING Hanging.

TRINKETS Bowie-knife and revolver.

TRISTIS Not good. "The fly kinchin is a tristis canis," the smart boy is a sad dog.

TROLL To loaf or loiter about.

TROT An old woman.

TROTTER-CASES Stockings.

TROTTERS Feet.

TRUCKS Pants.

TRUET Stealing money under pre-tense of changing it.

TRUMP A brave fellow.

TRUMPET A vain fellow who has a
decided partiality for the letter I.
TRUNDLERS Peas.
TRUNT Nose.
TRUNKER The body.
TRY ON To endeavor; attempt it.
"Coves who try on," fellows who live
by stealing.
TOGEMANDS A gown or cloak.
TWITTOCK Two.
TUMBLED Suspected; found it out.
"Tumbled on him," came upon him un-
expectedly. "Tumbled to him," sus-
pected him; thought it was him.
TUMBLER A cart; a lock; a sharper.
TUNE To beat. "Tune the toney,"
beat the fool.
TURF Race-course. "The knucks
work the turf for leather and skins,"
the pickpockets attend the race-courses
to steal pocket-books and purses.
TURKEY-MERCHANTS Purchasers
of stolen silk.
TURNED UP Acquitted; discharged.
TURNING OVER Examining.
TURTLE-DOVES A pair of gloves.
TWIG To observe. "Twig the copper,
he is peery," observe the officer, he is
watching us.
TWISTED Convicted, hanged.
TWO TO ONE A pawnbroker.
TYBURN BLOSSOM A young thief.
TYE A neckcloth.

TYKE A dog; a clown.

U

UNCLE A pawnbroker.

UNDER-DUBBER A turnkey.

UNICORN Two men and one woman, or two women and one man banded together to steal.

UNTRUSS To let down the shutters of a store.

UP HILLS False dice.

UPISH Testy; quarrelsome.

UPPER-BENJAMIN An overcoat.

UPRIGHT MAN King of the gipsies; the head of a gang of thieves; the chief of banditti.

UPRIGHTS Liquor measures.

UP THE SPOUT Pawned.

UP TO Knowing.

UP TO SLUM Humbug; gammon.

UP TO SNUFF Cunning; shrewd.

USED UP Killed; murdered.

U.S. COVE A soldier; a man in the employ of the United States.

U.S. PLATE Fetters; handcuffs.

V

VAG Vagrant. "Done on the vag," committed for vagrancy.

VAMOSE Run away; be off quick.

VAMP To pledge.

VAMPIRE A man who lives by extorting money from men and women whom they have seen coming out of or going into houses of assignation.

VAMPERS Stockings.

VARDY Opinion.

VELVET The tongue.

VENITE Come.

VENUS' CURSE Venereal disease.

VERGE A gold watch.

VICTUALLING OFFICE The stomach.

VINCENT'S LAW The art of cheating at cards.

VINEGAR A cloak or gown.

VIRTUE ATER A prostitute.

VIXEN A she-fox.

VOWEL Give your note; I.O.U.

W

WAITS Strolling musicians; organ-players, etc.

WALL-FLOWERS Second-hand clothing exposed for sale.

WAME The stomach.

WARE HAWK Look out; beware.

WARM Rich; plenty of money; dangerous.

WASTE A tavern.

WATERED Longed for. "The cove's chops watered for it," the fellow longed for it.

WATTLES The ears.

WEDGE Silver-ware.

WEDGE-BOX A silver snuff-box.

WEEDING Taking a part and leaving the balance in such a manner as not to excite suspicion. When a thief abstracts a portion from the plunder without the knowledge of his pals, and then receives an equal proportion of the remainder, it is called "Weeding the swag."

WELCHCOMB The thumb and finger.

WELL Not to divide fair; to conceal a part.

WESAND The throat.

WET-SNOW Wet linen.

WETTING Drinking.

WHACK Share of the plunder.

WHEEDLE To decoy a person by fawning or insinuation.

WHET To drink.

WHIDS Words. "Tip me your wattles, my pal, and touch my whids, or I'll make you whindle like a kinchin," give me your ears and take my words, or I'll make you snivel like a child.

WHIDDLE To tell or discover. "He whiddles," he peaches. "He whiddles the whole scrap," he tells all he knows. "The cull whiddled because they would not tip him his regulars," the fellow informed because they would not share with him. "The joskin whiddles beef, and we must pad the hoof," the countryman cries "thief," and we must be off.

WHIDDLER An informer; one who tells the secrets of another.

WHIFFLER A fellow that yelps or cries out with pain.

WHINDLE A low cry; a painful suppressed cry.

WHIPE A blow.

WHIPER A kerchief.

WHIP-JACKS Men who pretend to be shipwrecked sailors.

WHIPPED Cheated out of a share, or equal part of the plunder.

WHIPSTER A sharper; a cunning fellow.

WHISKER An enormous lie.

WHISKIN A drinking-vessel.

WHISTLER The throat.

WHIT A prison. "Five gonnoffs were rubbed in the darkmans out of the whit and piked like bulls into grassville," five thieves broke out of prison in the night, and ran like locomotives into the country.

WHITE TAPE Gin.

WHITE VELVET Gin.

WHITE WOOL Silver.

WIBBLE Bad drink.

WIFE A fetter fixed to one leg.

WIFFLER A relaxation.

WILD A village.

WILLOW Poor.

WIN A cent.

WIN To steal; to cheat. "The sneak tracked the dancers and win a twittock of witcher glimsticks," the thief went up-stairs and stole a pair of candlesticks.

WIND Money. "Raise the wind," get money.

WINDER To sentence for life. "The cove has napped a winder for settling a tony," the fellow has been sentenced for life for killing a fool.

WINGS Oars.

WINNINGS Plunder; money or goods.

WIRE A pickpocket; the fellow who picks the pocket.

WIREHOOK A pickpocket.

WISH Be off; away with you.

WITCHER Silver.

WITCHER BUBBER A silver bowl.

WOBALL A milkman.

WOBBLE To boil; to reel; to stagger.

WOOD In a quandary.

WOODBIRD A sheep.

WOODEN COAT A coffin.

WOODEN HABEAS A man who dies in prison is said to go out on a wooden habeas; that is, in his coffin.

WORD-PECKER A wit; a punster.

WORM To obtain knowledge by craft and cunning.

Y

YACK A watch.

YAM To eat.

YAVUM Bread and milk.

YELLOW Jealousy.

YELPER A fellow who cries before
he is hurt.

YIDISHER A Jew.

YOKED Married.

YOKLE A countryman.

Z

ZANY A jester.
ZNEES Ice; snow; frost.
ZOUCHER A slovenly fellow.
ZUCKE A dilapidated prostitute.

SCENE IN
A LONDON FLASH-
PANNY

"Ho! there, my rum-bluffer; send
me a nipperkin of white velvet."

"Make it two," said a woman, seat-
ing herself on a skinner's knee; "and if
Jim don't post the cole, I will."

"Why, Bell, is it yourself? Tip us
your daddle, my bene mort. May I
dance at my death, and grin in a glass-
case, if I didn't think you had been put
to bed with a shovel — you've been so
long away from the cock and hen
club."

"No, Jim, I only piked into
Deuceaville with a dimber-damber,
who couldn't pad the hoof for a single
darkman's without his bloss to keep
him from getting pogy."

"Oh! I'm fly. You mean Jumping
Jack, who was done last week, for
heaving a peter from a drag. But you

talked of padding the hoof. Why, sure, Jack had a rattler and a prad?"

"Yes, but they were spotted by the harmans, and so we walked Spanish."

"Was he nabbed on the scent?"

"No, his pal grew leaky and cackled."

"Well, Bell, here's the bingo — sluice your gob! But who was the cull that peached?"

"A slubber de gullion named Harry Long, who wanted to pass for an out-and-out cracksman, though he was merely a diver."

"Whew! I know the kiddy like a copper, and saved him once from lumping the lighter by putting in buck. Why, he scarcely knows a jimmy from a round robin, and Jack deserved the tippet for making a lay with him, as all coves of his kidney blow the gab. But how did you hare it to Romeville, Bell, for I suppose the jets cleaned you out?"

"I kidded a swell in a snoozing-ken, and shook him of his dummy and thimble."

"Ah! Bell! you were always the blowen for a rum bing."

"It was no great quids, Jim — only six flimseys and three beans. But I'm flush of the balsam now, for I dance balum-rancum for the bens."

Bell here produced a rum bing, which at once made her popular, and the nucleus of a host of admirers; for, as it respects money, it is with rogues and their doxeys as with all the rest of the world. Bell truly justified the adage, that "What's got over the devil's back, goes under the devil's belly;" for she gave a general order to the rumbluffer, to supply all the lush that was called for by the company, at her expense; and thereon there was a demand for max, oil of barby, red tape, blue ruin, white velvet, and so forth, that kept all the tapsters in the establishment in a state of restless activity for the next half-hour.

"Bell, you're benish to-night," exclaimed Knapp, who probably had a design on the purse, which the course of events somewhat interfered with.

"Stubble your red rag," answered a good looking young fellow. "Bell had better flash her dibs than let you bubble her out of them."

"Why, you joskin," retorted Jim; "if you don't stow your whids I'll put your bowsprit in parenthesis. Ogle the cove, Bell — he wants to pass for a snafler in his belcher tye, though he never bid higher than a wipe in an upper benjamin."

"I may bid as high as your pintle, and make you squint like a bag of nails," replied the intruder, "though you rub us to whit for it."

"Oh, it's all plummy," said Knapp, "so you may cly your daddles. But come, Bell, let us track the dancers and rumble the flats, for I'm tired of pattering flash and lushing jackey."

"Bar that toss, Jim," said Bell, "for you're as fly at the pictures, as the devil at lying, and I would rather be a knight of Alsatia than a plucked pigeon."

This resolution produced a round of applause, which was followed by another round of liquor — promptly paid for by the lady of the rum bing, whose generosity now so far extended itself, that she withdrew from Mr. Knapp's protection, and, even without waiting to be asked, deposited herself in the lap of him of the belcher tye. She had scarcely asserted her title to the premises, before it was disputed by another fair damsel, who emphatically declared, that if the tenant in possession did not immediately leave that, she would astonish her mazzard with the contents of a "nipper-kin of thunder and lightning."

"If you do," returned Bell, "I will fix my diggers in your dial-plate, and turn it up with red."

"Mizzle, you punk."

"Well said, Madame Rhan, but the bishop might as soon call the parson pig-stealer."

"You lie, you bat. I couple with no cove but my own. But say, Harry, will you suffer yourself to be made a two-legged stool of by a flag-about?"

"Oh! button your bone-box, Peg," replied Harry. "Bell's a rum blowen, and you only patter because your ogle's as green as the Emerald Isle."

"It's not half so green as yourself, halter-mad Harry," retorted Peg; "for you know if I wished to nose I could have you twisted — not to mention any thing about the cull that was hushed for his reader."

On a bench, close by the last speaker, was seated Hitch, a police officer, who appeared to be quite at home with the company, and to occasion no alarm or misgivings; but the moment Peg mentioned the circumstance of "the cull that was hushed for his reader," he rose from the table, drew forth a pair of handcuffs, and tapping Knapp's rival on the shoulder, playfully whispered:

"Harry, my lad, the game's up;
hold out your wrists for the ruffles."

"There they are, Mr. Hitch, though
I suppose you'll be asking me in a
week or so to hold out my gorge for a
Tyburn tippet."

These proceedings naturally drew a
crowd around the parties concerned;
but though all sympathized with the
prisoner, and the minion of the law
was without any assistant, yet there
was not the slightest attempt at a res-
cue, or even the least disposition mani-
fested by the captive of a desire to
escape.

"Only nine months on the pad, and
to be up for scragging! What a pity!"

"He's too young — he hasn't had
his lark half out; and it's like making a
man pay a debt he don't owe, to twist
him before he has gone the rounds."

"He'll die game for all that! Poor
fellow! he takes it like a glass of egg-
nog."

"Ah! Mr. Hitch! isn't it out of order, and he so green? You ought to
give a chap a year to ripen for the
hemp."

"Do, Hitch, give him a little longer
rope, and take him in his regular turn.
You're sure to have him, you known,
when his time's up."

"O! stubble it, George. Hitch can't, or he would; for he never hurries a cove when it's left to himself."

"That's a fact, my kiddies," exclaimed the officer, who seemed pleased at the compliment; "but the commissioner wants Harry, and so, of course, I must pull him."

"I'm satisfied, whatever comes of it," added the prisoner.

Bell whispered in the officer's ear: "Couldn't you let him pike if I come down with a thimble and ten beans?"

"A watch and ten guineas?"

"Of course."

"I might if you paid on delivery."

"Ready's the word."

"Warehawk, then, and follow."

Hitch departed with his prisoner, followed by Bell; but in a few minutes the latter returned and whispered to Knapp:

"Your client has slipped the darbys, and his name's Walker. Here's a flimsy, to lay low and bottle your gab."

The flash-panny was now in the full tide of successful operation — two thirds of its patrons being about three sheets in the wind, and none of them perfectly sober. In one corner there was a mill, wherein the combatants hit the wall more frequently than they hit each other. In another, two blowens were clapper-clawing each other for a bob-cull, who was seconding both parties, and declaring that the winner should have him. Here a snafler lay snoring on a bench, while a buzman, just half a degree less intoxicated, was endeavoring to pick his pocket. There, three cracksmen were engaged in a remarkably animated dispute on the state of the country. Under almost every table might be seen a son or daughter of Adam, luxuriating in the realms of Nod. But the bulk of the company were amusing themselves in a dance; for one of the fixtures of the establishment was an Irish piper, who, by the way, was a little fortune to it, for every one treated Pat.

The dance was yet in its fullest vigor, when Hitch returned and called Bell to one of the tables.

"Bell, said he, "I have been looking for you more eagerly than any of your lovers for several months past — though I found you at length by an accident. What have you done with the bloke?"

"Me, Hitch? Why, I have neither seen or heard of him."

"Come, Bell, it's no use our wasting time in small talk. You were with him the last night he was heard of."

"Not I, faith, Hitch. Bring me the book, and I'll swear No to that."

"How then came you by his super?"

"Blast the super! for I fear it has got me into a muss."

"If I take you to Newgate for it, Bell, it will be apt to get you into a halter."

"Well, then it will save me from the Bay fever, or dying in the gutter; for all such as I am must draw one of the three chances."

"Make me your confessor, Bell, without any equivocation or drawback, and I may stand between you and Jack Ketch."

"But what about the stone-jug?"

"That depends upon circumstances. Is the bloke living or dead?"

"Living, for all I know to the contrary."

"You know all about him, Bell."

"If I do, may I cly the jerk at a drag; be trussed in a Kilmainham garter, and fall to the surgeons."

"Well, it may be so," said Hitch, musing; "for if you knew all, half the world would have known it before this time. However, Bell, you can supply a link or two in the chain of evidence, so give me the particulars; and remember, if you tell me a lie I will smell it as it comes out of your mouth."

160

Just then the guests of the Crooked Billet were interrupted by an uproar in the street.

"Some swells on a lark," exclaimed lawyer Knapp; "dub the jigger and let them in."

And Jim was right; for on the jigger being dubbed, in staggered four bloods, who were sufficiently top-heavy to be ready for any thing. Two of the newcomers, who prided themselves on "knowing the ropes," while their companions were green from the fens. Immediately on their entrance, this hopeful addition to the convivial party already assembled, began to exhibit their "tip-top education" by squaring off for a fight, pattering flash, and ordering in lush. In fact, they out-heroded Herod, for they proved themselves to be yet greater blackguards than the poor rogues whom they were so emulous to imitate. And yet they were "gentlemen," who would have been shocked at the touch of a mechanic, though they gloried in doing things up nutty, like pickpockets and highway men. But they were not such knowing kiddies after all, though they considered themselves bang up to the mark; for suddenly one of them cried out that he had lost his purse; and then they all discovered that they had lost everything they had which was fairly removable. Thereupon there was a devil of a muss, generally, with vociferous calling for the police. The four fellows who had the four worst hats, exchanged them *sans ceremonie* with the strangers, while a couple of foglehunters tore off the skirts of their coats to mend their breeches. To finish their spree, by and by in rushed the police, and, on the charge of an elderly, responsible-looking cracksman, hurried the bloods off to the nearest stationhouse. What rascally things are policemen! Alas! and alack! just about as rascally as all the rest of the world.

Numeration

1. On.
2. Duo.
3. Tray.
4. Quatre.
5. Cink or Finniff.
6. Double Tray.
7. A Round.
8. Double Quarter.
9. A Floorer.
10. Double Finiff.

Examples

Tim Sullivan buzzed a bloke and a shakester of a reader. His jomer stalled. Johnny Miller, who was to have his regulars, called out, "cop-bung," for as you see a fly-cop was marking. Jack speeled to the crib, when he found Johnny Doyle had been pulling down sawney for grub. He cracked a casa last night, and fenced the swag. He told Jack as how Bill had flimped a yack, and pinched a swell of a spark-fawney, and had sent the yack to church, and got half a century and a finnif for the fawney.

Translation

Tim Sullivan picked the pockets of a gentleman and lady of a pocket-book and purse. Tim's fancy-girl stood near him and screened him from observation. Johnny Miller, who was to have a share of the plunder, called out to him: "Hand over the stolen property — a detective is observing your manoeuvres." Sullivan ran immediately to his house, when he found Johnny Doyle had provided something to eat, by stealing some bacon from a store-door. Doyle committed a burglary last night, and disposed of the property plundered. He told Sullivan that Bill had hustled a person, and obtained a watch, and also robbed a well-dressed gentleman of a diamond ring. The watch he sent to have the works taken out and put into another case, or the maker's name erased and another inserted; the ring realized him fifty-five dollars.

Appendix

The Gambler's Flash

WORDS FREQUENTLY USED BY
GAMBLERS AMONG THEM-
SELVES, SOMETIMES IN GEN-
ERAL CONVERSATION, AND
SOMETIMES WHILE AT PLAY.

A

A GOSS The card that has won three
times in one deal.

ANTI-GOSS The card that has lost
three times in one deal. It is sometimes
called a "hotel." For instance, a gambler who has been playing, finally gets
"broke;" but the love of play which
from habit has become a second nature
in him, causes him to linger behind to
see the luck of others at the table. Being "dead broke," he borrows from a
brother gambler money enough to pay
his hotel or boarding-house bill. While

looking on at the game an anti-goss occurs, and thinking that the fourth time
is sure to win, he stakes the money he
has borrowed to pay the hotel, boarding-house, or washerwoman's bill,
whichever it may be, and he loses. The
exclamation among gamblers would be
then, "There goes his hotel."

ARTIST   One who excels as a gamester.

B

BANK   Without a party to play
against, there can be no faro-playing.
The player must play against some
body, and that some body is a party of
one or more, who hire rooms, and own
gambling instruments. The gambling
concern is owned by them, and the servants, from the negro at the door who
answers to the touch of the bell, to the
gentlemanly "picker-up," are in their
pay, and act entirely in accordance
with their instructions. The capital
which the owners invest in this gambling co-partnership is called the
"bank," but the amount varies greatly.
Some banking concerns are not worth
over $100, while others are worth
$100,000. It is sometimes easy to
break a bank of limited capital, but to
make bankrupt the other is almost an

impossibility. The necessity of a large capital is apparent. If four or six parties seated at the table should have $50 each on the table, and four of the six should win and the other two lose, then the bank in five minutes could be $1000 the loser. The bank must be always prepared to lose a thousand or two of an evening, they knowing well enough that it will all come back to them before the game closes.

BANKER The man who puts the money up to be played for. The owner of the bank.

BETTER A party who enters a gambling-saloon, takes his seat at the table, and commences to play, is a better.

BETTING ON TIME This frequently occurs when the character of a party is such that he can be trusted to pay the money he borrows or the debts he incurs. If his character is good in this respect, then he will be permitted to play after he is "broke," if it occurs that he should be the loser when he rises from the table. This is betting on time. The same thing is done in Wall street every day by speculating brokers. In Wall street gambling there are the "bulls" and the "bears," the object of the one being to raise stock above its actual value and then dispose of it, while the other party depresses it below its value

168

and then purchases it. Nothing of this
sort, however, occurs among the professional gamblers, who locate in
Broadway and some of the down-town
streets running from it.

C

CALLING THE TURN When there is
one turn, say 4, 6, and 8, and the
player calls 4, 8, the caller loses; but if
on the other hand it should be the cards
he calls, then he wins, and is paid four
to one. When a man calls both, he
wins and loses on the same turn. In the
last turn the player can win three ways.
He can copper, call, and play the winning card. He can double the limit of
the game, which is the privilege of the
player on the last turn.
CAPPER A man who sits at the table
and plays, but neither wins nor loses.
He is there only for the purpose of
swelling the number of players, so that
the game won't hurry through too
quickly, thus giving the actual player
proper time to consider the game and
study the moves he should make.
CAPPER A man in the employ of the
bank, who pretends to be playing
against it, and winning large amounts.
Some gambling-houses in New-York
keep two sets of cappers all the time;

one set goes on at ten in the morning and retires at six in the evening, when the night-set comes on. Thus the game is continually going on; no matter when a man entered, he finds the game in full blast, and there never is any necessity to start it because of a fresh arrival. Professional gamblers drop to cappers very quickly. Cappers usually want to make too big bets — that is, make too heavy bets. As a general thing they want to bet with the red checks, which represent $5, putting down ten or twenty at a time.

CASHING This is getting the money from the bank for the checks or chips, if the player has any left on hand when he stops playing.

CAT HOPP Is when there is one turn left in the box of the same denomination. For instance, two jacks and a five; or three cards in the box, and two of a similar count.

CHANGING IN Handing in your money for the chips.

CHIPS or CHECKS The chips or checks are round fancy pieces of ivory of the size of a half dollar, and a trifle thicker. These represent money, and are received from the dealer to play with in exchange for money. They are much easier to handle, and the dealer can see at a glance how much money is bet on a card. The color of the chips indicate the value they represent. There are three colors, namely, white, red and blue. White chips represent twenty-five cents, or one dollar, according to the house. Red chips represent five times the value of the white chips. Blue chips represent $25, $50, and $100. A hundred dollar chip is the highest "fish", as the gambler calls it.

CHOPPING A card which commences to win and lose alternately, is called chopping, and to commence to lose and win alternately, is anti-chopping.

COLD DECK This is generally done in short cards, or short games. A pack of cards is shuffled, and just as they are about to be dealt out, another pack is substituted. This is sometimes done by faro-players. The dealer having shuffled the cards, or having got another party to do it, drops the cards at his feet, and lifts the packed cards from a handkerchief on his lap. He calls on Sambo, the darkey waiter, to lift a check at his feet, and thus the evidence of his guilt is carried off unobserved. When cleverly done, the trick can not be discovered. One gambler often plays this trick on another, and hence it derives the expressive name of "cold deck."

COPPER A card can be played to win or lose, at the option of the player. If he wishes to play any particular card to lose, he places a penny on top of the money he stakes. This signifies that he plays it to lose; hence it is called coppering.

CRAPS or PROPS A game peculiar to Boston. Sometimes it is played with shells, and sometimes with coffee-beans, but more generally the former, as they can be loaded. If four shells are not at hand, four coffee-beans answer the same purpose. It is a substitute for the dice. Thousands of dollars have been lost on this game, but as it has not received the same condemnation from the moral portion of the community that dice has, Bostonians patronize it. There is no other reason why that city alone should patronize it. The game is so childish, that it is ten times more dangerous than any other, and gamblers have no trouble in "roping in" men to play at it, who would faint with horror at the sight of a pack of cards.

CUE Is a calculation which confirmed gamblers are guided altogether by in playing. They know that after three cards of one denomination have gone out, they can not be split.

CUE-BOX The cue-box is an exact representation of the lay-out of the cards on the table. The player, by looking at the cue-box, can instantly see what cards have been drawn from the box, thus relieving him of the trouble of keeping the run of the cards in his head. For instance if four jacks had been drawn from the box, and a player should place his money on the jack, they being all drawn, he could not win or lose.

CUE-KEEPER The man who keeps the cues or marks, so that a player knows by looking at it, which card is in and which is out.

D

DEALER The party who deals out the cards, receiving generally for his services from ten to twenty per cent of the profits of the game from the banker.

DOUBLE CARD Two cards of the same denomination.

E

EVEN The player who trys to make up what he has lost. Having lost $50, he stakes another $50, perhaps his last, for the purpose of getting back what he had lost, to be even with the bank, or get broke in the attempt.

F

FLAT One who has no knowledge, or
an imperfect knowledge, of gambling.
No matter how much a man may know
of all the sciences in the world, if he is
ignorant of gambling, and should enter
a gambling-room, the players would
smile and say, "There's a flat," a man
who did not know any thing.

G

GAFF The gaff is a ring worn on the
fore-finger of the dealer. It has a sharp
point on the inner side, and the gambler, when dealing from a two-card
box, can deal out the card he chooses;
some, however, are smart enough to
do this trick without the gaff. It is now
out of date, and the only city in which
it is now in use, is Baltimore. The gaff
has been the initiative idea of tricks of
this character, and many improve-
ments, of which it is the foundation,
have been discovered by sharpers.

H

HOCK The last card in the box.
Among thieves a man is in hock when
he is in prison; but when one gambler
is caught by another, smarter than him-

self, and is beat, then he is in hock.
Men are only caught, or put in hock,
on the race-tracks, or on the steam-
boats down South. In a hock-game, if a
man hits a card, he is obliged to let his
money lie until it either wins or loses.
Of course there are nine hundred and
ninety-nine chances against the player,
and the oldest man living never yet saw
him win, and thus he is caught in hock.

I

ITEMS Items derives his name from
looking at a party's hand, and conveying to the opposition player what it con-
tains by signs. This is Item's
occupation. A looking-glass is sometimes used, sometimes signs which
mutes would only understand, and
sometimes the signs are agreed upon
and known only to the parties inter-
ested.

L

LAMAS High chips or checks repre-
senting $25, $50, and $100. There are
no $1000 lamas, for the simple reason
that with $100 chips any amount of
money can be laid on the table.

LAY-OUT The "lay-out" is composed of all the cards in a suit, commencing at the ace and ending at the king. These cards are posted upon a piece of velvet, which can be spread upon the table whenever the dealer chooses to open the game. When play has commenced, each player places his stake upon any card he may choose, and as the cards are drawn from the box, his bet is determined.

LEAVING OUT When a dispute arises, a referee of outsiders or lookers-on, is appointed, to whom the difficulty is referred, and whose decision among professional men is decisive.

LITTLE FIGURE Ace, deuce, and tray.

LOOK-OUT The look-out is the man who is supposed to keep every thing straight, and see that no mistake is made, and that the dealer does not neglect to lift any money that he has won.

M

MARKER Marking is frequently done in playing the game of faro. It is something put down on the card, a pencil, a knife, or any thing, to represent any amount of money the player pleases. He says: I bet $5, $10, $50, or $100, as it suits him and his finances. This saves him from delaying the game by going through his pockets for the exact money he wants. When the deal is out, he settles.

N

NUDGE This is not often practised at the game of faro; it is applicable, as its name implies, to cribbage and similar games. The office of a nudger is to touch an associate with his feet. These touchings are signs, which are denominated nudging.

P

PALMING Concealing cards in the palm of the hands.

PARLIEU Is to allow one's money to lie on the table and double. For instance, the player puts $5 on the table, and it wins; instead of lifting it, he lets the original sum lie — that is called a parlieu.

PICKER-UP We frequently read of country-men being "roped" into gambling-houses, but this occurs from the ignorance of the reporters, who know nothing of the language used by gamblers and sportsmen. Gamblers of the higher grade in New-York, never use

the word "roper-in." It is usually confi-
dence-men, ball-players, pocket book
droppers, and others attacked to that
fraternity. The roper-in takes a man
over to Brooklyn or New-Jersey, and is
an actor in the swindle; the picker-up
takes his man to a gambling-saloon,
and there leaves him to be enchanted,
enchained, and allured by what he
sees. Sometimes he only gives the man
he has picked up his card, which will
admit him to a gaming-house, where
he can play a card of another descrip-
tion. The roper-in and the picker-up
therefore should not be confounded.

The picker-up is always a gentleman, in manners, taste, dress, and ap-
pearance, and sometimes has the
superficial knowledge of a scholar. He
is thoroughly informed on all the topics
of the day. He has seen New-Orleans,
knows all about it, and can talk of the
gallant defense made there from behind
the cotton-bales. He knows all about
the evil results arising out of the agita-
tion of the slavery question. He loves
Boston and New-England, for it was
there he was born and spent his earliest
and his happiest days; it was the cradle
and the birth-place of liberty, and the
world looked with unreserved delight
upon the efforts which the men of the
East put forth in the cause of freedom;

he has spent many happy years in the far West, its vast prairies, its widespread, majestic forests, and mighty rivers, and he can not help warming up when he reverts to these themes, which moved the hearts of philosophers, poets, and statesmen.

This is the picker-up. He first sees the man's name on the hotel-register, and where he is from. He then sees him out, studies his character, and ascertains his means and the object of his visit to the city; and the picker-up, if smart, reads his victim phrenologically without touching his head. Every man has some weak point which can be played upon, and the duty of the picker-up is to discover it. It does not take him long generally to get a stranger to visit a gambling-hall. Very many of the servants of hotels are in the pay of pickers-up — the duty of the servant being to get information concerning guests, which his employer can use.

PIKER Is a man who plays very small amounts. Plays a quarter, wins, pockets the winnings, and keeps at quarters; and never, if he can help it, bets on his winnings.

PLAYING ON VELVET Playing on the money that has been won from the bank.

PRESS When a man wins a bet, and instead of lifting and pocketing the winnings, he adds to the original stake and winnings, it becomes a press.

PRIVATE GAME So called because the flat is led to suppose that no professional gamblers are admitted, and thus he is the more easily duped.

PUBLIC GAME A game where any body can be admitted.

R

REPEATER For instance, when a card wins or loses at one deal, and the same thing occurs the next deal, it is a repeater.

ROUNDER One who hangs around faro-banks, but does not play. In other words, a loafer, a man who travels on his shape, and is supported by a woman, but does not receive enough money to enable him to play faro. Gamblers call such men rounders, outsiders, loafers.

RUSSER A big player.

S

SHOE-STRING When a man bets a small amount and runs it up to a large amount, it is called a shoe-string.

SHORT CARDS By some called short game. A game of seven-up or cribbage. For instance, "Have you been playing faro to-night?" "No." "What then?" "I have been playing short cards."

SLEEPER A bet won by the bank or a better, which has been overlooked and lies on the table without a claimant.

SKINNING A sure game, where all who play are sure to lose, except the gamesters.

SPLIT When two cards come alike. For instance, if two jacks should come out, the banker takes one half of the money.

SQUARE GAME When cards are dealt fairly, and there is no cheating.

SUMMER GAME Playing merely for amusement.

SUMMER GAME Playing a game for the benefit of another person with his money.

STRIPPERS Cards cut at the sides for the purpose of carrying on a skinning game.

STUCK When a man has lost all his money, and is trying on the last throw to retrieve his loss and he is beat, then he is stuck.

SUCKER A flat; one who can play cards, but does not know all the tricks and traps in gambling.

SUPPER CUSTOMERS Some of the fashionable gambling-houses have free suppers for their customers; this is done to induce the better class of gambling merchants to patronize the house. But there are some men who frequent these houses and take supper, but never play. When such a one is asked if he is going to take a hand in, his usual answer is, "Thank you, sir, I'm a supper customer to night."

T

TELL-BOX The tell-box is an improvement on the gaff, and has a fine spring attached to it. The object is to cheat the dealer. The dealer plays with a pack of cards which the player has had a chance to handle, and he rubs the backs of certain of them with sand-paper. The rough card adheres to the smooth one, and the fact that it does not move a hair's breadth in the box enables him to know the card that is covered, and he plays accordingly. He can also play in the same manner with a new pack of cards without sanding them, as certain cards require a greater amount of ink than others.

THE POT The six, seven, and eight.

TRICKS When a player takes the cards from his opponent that counts. If

the queen is put down and the king follows, which is higher, then the queen
is taken. That is a trick.

TRICK GAMES Such games as whist,
where tricks count.

Z

ZODIAC This word has degenerated
into Soda. It means the top card in the
box.

TECHNICAL WORDS AND
PHRASES,
USED BY

BILLIARD-PLAYERS

ATTITUDE The position in which the
player stands while at the billiard-table,
when about to strike the ball. The ac-
quisition of a good attitude is a matter
of first importance to the new begin-
ner. It is almost impossible to lay down
fixed rules in this particular, as the pe-
culiarities of height and figure would
render the rules that would be excellent
in one case, totally inapplicable in the
other. Perfect ease is the grand *desid-
eratum;* and this is to be acquired by

practice, and a close observation of the best players.

BANK When the player makes his own ball hit any of the cushions before striking the object-ball.

BILLIARD-SHARP A class of character not tolerated in respectable saloons. As a general thing, the billiard-sharp is a retired marker, who fancies it is no longer respectable to work for an honest living, but that he is smart enough, and has learned tricks enough at his former business, to enable him to win as much money as he wants from the less experienced amateurs of the game, who figure in his vocabulary as "the flats." He generally frequents those establishments where one or two billiard-tables are made the stall behind which some dishonest occupation is carried on; and here he is at home, and in his glory. He makes himself particularly friendly with any one who will ask him to "take a drink," and in his assumed duties he fills the offices of lounger, runner, talker, player, sponge, shoulder-hitter, and referee.

He is also a runner, and sort of travelling blower to second-rate manufacturers of billiard-tables. These men supply him with clothes, to enable him to mingle in respectable society, and allow him an enormous per centage for every billiard-table sold to a stranger through his agency. In addition to this, it is his business to pull down the reputation of such manufacturers as despise and scorn the means by which he earns his dishonest livelihood. As soon as he has made "a hit" in one saloon, he is off to another, and in this way goes the rounds of the city until all the places which harbor him, are, in his own phrase, "played out."

Such a man is to be avoided as one of the worst species of sharpers. He has a thousand pretenses under which to borrow money, and will act as if quite offended if refused. The stranger should avoid all such men, and especially any one with whom he is not well acquainted, who should ask him to play for any given sum, "just to give an interest to the game."

BOWERY SHOT When the balls played with and at, are jarred together — a pushing shot.

BREAK The position the balls are left in after the shot.

BURST A term chiefly used at pinpool, when a player has exceeded the number which is placed as the common limit to the game, and must, therefore, either retire from the game, or take a privilege of another life.

CAROM (French, *Carambolage*) To hit more than one of the balls on the table with your own. In England this word has been corrupted to "cannon."

COUNT Is the reckoning of the game. Making a count, is to make a stroke which will add some figures to the player's reckoning.

DISCOUNT When one player is so much the superior of another, that he allows all the counts made by his opponent to be deducted from his own reckoning, he is said to "discount" his adversary's gains. In "double" and "treble discounts," twice and thrice the amount of his opponent's gains are deducted from the player's score. In no other game but billiards are such immense odds possible. A man of close observation, temperate habits, steady nerves, and large experience, may gave almost any odds to an inferior player, and still have a fair chance of success.

DOUBLET or CROSS When the ball to be pocketed is first made to rebound from the opposite cushion.

FOLLOW When a player's ball rolls on after another ball which it has impelled forward.

FORCE When the player's ball retrogrades after coming in contact with another.

FOUL STROKE or SHOT Any stroke made in violation of the known rules of the game.

FULL BALL, QUARTER BALL, HALF BALL, FINE or CUT BALL, OWN OR CUE BALL, and OBJECT BALL The "object ball" is the ball aimed at; the "own or cue ball" is the ball directed toward the "object ball;" the other terms relate to the position in which the object ball is struck.

GERMANTOWNER *See Bowery Shot.*

HAZARD To drive any of the balls into any of the pockets.

HAZARD, DOUBLE When two balls are pocketed with the same stroke.

HAZARD, LOSING When the player's ball is pocketed by his own act.

HAZARD, WINNING When the player pockets either of the red balls, or his adversary's ball.

HAZARD, TAKING A   A term used to express that a player is so confident of making a certain hazard, that he will undertake to do it, under penalty of los-ing, in case he does not succeed, as many lives as he would have gained if successful. The phrase is most fre-quently employed in two-ball pool.

HUG When any of the balls run close alongside of a particular cushion, they are said to hug it.

JAW When a ball is prevented from dropping into a pocket by the cushions, which extend like jaws on either side.

JUMP When the player forces his ball by a downward stroke to leap up from the table.

KILLED or DEAD BALL When a ball in pool has lost its lives, and its chances are not renewed by privileges, it is said to be killed.

KISS When the ball played with strikes another ball more than once, they are said to kiss; or when two balls, not played with, come in contact.

LONE GAME A game in which one of the parties is an experienced player, and the other a novice — the former having the game in his own hands.

MISS To fail striking any of the balls upon the table.

MISS-CUE When the cue, from any cause, slips off the ball without accomplishing the intended stroke.

PLAYING FOR SAFETY When the player foregoes a possible advantage, in order to leave the balls in such a position that his opponent can make nothing out of them.

PLAYING SPOT BALL When the player is not limited to the number of times he may pocket the red ball from the spot.

PRIVILEGE When a player loses the lives, or chances, which were given to his ball on its entry into the game, and desires to purchase another chance from the other players, he asks a "privilege."

SCRATCH When a player wins a stroke or count by accident, without deserving it, he is said to have made a scratch.

STRINGING FOR THE LEAD A preliminary arrangement, by which it is determined who shall have the choice of lead and balls.

TIMBER LICK *See Bowery Shot.*

Brokers'
technicalities in brief

A BULL is one who buys stocks on speculation, thinking they will rise, so that he can sell at a profit.

A BEAR is one who sells stocks on speculation, thinking they will fall, so that he can buy in for less money to fill his contracts.

A CORNER is when the bears can not buy or borrow the stock to deliver in fulfillment of their contracts.

A DEPOSIT is earnest-money lodged in the hands of a third party, as a guaranty; "5 up," "10 up," etc., is the language expressive of a deposit.

OVERLOADED is when the bulls can not pay for the stocks they have purchased.

SHORT is when a person or party sells stocks when they have none, and expect to buy or borrow them in time to deliver.

LONG is when a person or party has a
plentiful supply of stocks.

A FLYER is to buy some stock with a
view to selling it in a few days, and
either make or lose, as luck will have it.

A WASH is a pretended sale, by special agreement between the seller and
buyer, for the purpose of getting a quo-
tation reported.

A HUNDRED
STRETCHES HENCE

OH! where will be the culls of the bing
    A hundred stretches hence?
The bene morts, who sweetly sing,
    A hundred stretches hence?
The autum-cacklers, autum-coves,
The jolly blade who wildly roves;
And where the buffer, bruiser, blowen,
And all the cops and beaks so knowin',
    A hundred stretches hence?

And where the swag, so bleakly
pinched,
    A hundred stretches hence?
The thimbles, slang, and danglers
filched,
    A hundred stretches hence?
The chips, the fawneys, chatty-feeders,
The bugs, the boungs, and well-filled
readers;
And where the fence and snoozing-ken,
With all the prigs and lushing men,
    A hundred stretches hence?

Played out their lay, it will be said
    A hundred stretches hence,
With shovels they were put to bed
    A hundred stretches since!
Some rubbed to whit had napped a win-
der,
And some were scragged and took a
blinder,
Planted the swag, and lost to sight,
We'll bid them, one and all, good
night,
    A hundred stretches hence.

Technical words and phrases in general use by Pugilists

ABROAD Confused; staggered.

A GENERAL Possessed of superior science.

BACK-HANDED BLOW Striking with the back of the clenched fist.

BARNEY A fight that is sold.

BEAK The nose.

BEAM-ENDS Thrown or knocked into a sitting position.

BOKO The nose.

BOTTOM Power of endurance.

BOUNCED Frightened with stories of another's prowess.

BREAD-BASKET The stomach.

BUFFER A pugilist.

CHANCERY When one boxer gets the head of his opponent under his left arm, and holding him by the left wrist, strikes him in the face with his right hand, severely punishing him.

CLARET Blood.

CHOPPER A blow given from above.

COLORS The respective handkerchiefs that each fights under.

COMMISSARY The person who fixes the ropes and stakes.

CONK The nose.

CORINTHIAN CANVAS A term applied to the *propria personae* of an English nobleman who is an amateur of pugilism.

COUNTER-HITTING When both parties in a fight strike each other at the same time.

CROSS-BUTTOCK To get an adversary on the hip, and then throw him.

CUT OF TIME Defeated; could not come up to the call.

DADDLES The hands.

DOING WORK Training.

DOUBLER A blow which causes the person struck to bend forward.

DUKES The hands.

DUTCH COURAGE Cowardice; one who drinks liquor to stimulate his courage.

ENOUGH When one of the boxers wishes to discontinue the fight he exclaims, "Enough."

FACER A severe blow struck directly in the face.

FEINTING Making pretense of delivering a blow.

FIBBING Short, quick blows when the parties are close to each other.

FIDDLER A pugilist that depends more upon his activity than upon his bottom.

FINICKING FOP A dandy or empty swell who makes much ado about pugilism, because he thinks it knowing and stylish.

FINE FETTLE In good condition; healthy.

FLABBY The flesh in a soft condition.

FLOORER A knock down blow.

FORKS The hands.

FOSSED Thrown.

FOUL An unwarrantable interference on the part of a second to frustrate an opponent's designs.

FOUL BLOW A blow given contrary to the accepted rules of the ring; below the belt.

GAME Courageous, unflinching.

GAVE IN Yielded.

GLUTTONY Punishing a man severely, without special regard to the science of pugilism. One who can endure a great amount of punishment is called a *glutton*.

GOB The mouth.

GOOD-WOOLED A man of unflinching courage.

GOT HOME A telling blow.

GROGGY Not able to stand erect from punishment received.

GRUEL Punishment.

GULLET The throat.

HIGH-COLORING Drawing blood freely.

IN DIFFICULTIES Nearly defeated.

IN MOURNING The eyes blackened and closed up.

IN TROUBLE Almost beaten.

IVORIES Teeth.

JOLLYING Low expressions used by one combatant to the other during the fight, for the purpose of irritating him and diverting his attention.

KNOWLEDGE-BOX The head.

LAMPS The eyes.

LEARY Active; smart.

LEVELLER When one of the contestants is brought completely to the ground.

LISTENERS The ears.

MARK The pit of the stomach.

MAZZARD The mouth.

MENTOR A second in the ring.

MILLED *See Punished.*

MILLING COVES Persons who regularly frequent milling-pannies, for the purpose of exhibiting their skill in boxing.

MILLING-PANNIES Places of resort for pugilists in which sparring exhibitions are given.

MITTENS Boxing-gloves.

MITTEN-MILL A glove fight.

MUSH The mouth.

NUT The head.

NUT-CRACKER A severe blow on the head.

OGLES The eyes.

PINS The legs.

PLUCK Spirit; boldness; courage.

POTATO-TRAP The mouth.

PUFFED Swollen.

PUNISHED Severely bruised or cut in the fight.

RALLY When the fighters close up and strike promiscuously.

RANTER One who makes greater pretension of skill in boxing than he exhibits when engaged in a set-to.

RIB-BENDER A forcible hit in the ribs.

RUBY Blood.

SHAKE-UP A pugilistic encounter.

SHIFT When a boxer purposely falls to save himself from a knock-down blow, he is said to make a *shift*.

SLOGGER A pugilist.

SMELLER The nose.

SPARRING GILLS *See Milling Coves.*

STAMINA Ability to punish and endure punishment.

TAKE THE SHINE OUT To lower the man's self-esteem.

THE CROOK Entwining the legs for a fall.

THE SCRATCH A line drawn in the middle of the ring.

THREW DOWN THE GLOVE Gave a challenge.

TIME The breathing-space which, by the accepted rules of the ring, is confined to a given period. "Coming to time," is coming promptly to the line at the expiration of the time agreed upon.

TOLD OUT Beaten; defeated.

UPPER CUT A terrific blow struck upwards.

UPPER CUSTOMER A term applied to patrons of the ring amongst the upper classes who are not themselves pugilists.

UPPER STORY The head.

WHITE FEATHER Cowardice.

WIND UP The finishing round.

COSIMO is a specialty publisher of books and publications that inspire, inform, and engage readers. Our mission is to offer unique books to niche audiences around the world.

COSIMO BOOKS publishes books and publications for innovative authors, nonprofit organizations, and businesses. **COSIMO BOOKS** specializes in bringing books back into print, publishing new books quickly and effectively, and making these publications available to readers around the world.

COSIMO CLASSICS offers a collection of distinctive titles by the great authors and thinkers throughout the ages. At **COSIMO CLASSICS** timeless works find new life as affordable books, covering a variety of subjects including: Business, Economics, History, Personal Development, Philosophy, Religion & Spirituality, and much more!

COSIMO REPORTS publishes public reports that affect your world, from global trends to the economy, and from health to geopolitics.

FOR MORE INFORMATION CONTACT US AT
INFO@COSIMOBOOKS.COM

✹ if you are a book lover interested in our current catalog of books

✹ if you represent a bookstore, book club, or anyone else interested in special discounts for bulk purchases

✹ if you are an author who wants to get published

✹ if you represent an organization or business seeking to publish books and other publications for your members, donors, or customers.

**COSIMO BOOKS ARE ALWAYS
AVAILABLE AT ONLINE BOOKSTORES**

VISIT COSIMOBOOKS.COM
BE INSPIRED, BE INFORMED

CPSIA information can be obtained at www.ICGtesting.com
Printed in the USA
LVOW06s0745101013

356136LV00001B/52/P